Potato Branch

JOE RICHARD MORGAN

Potato Branch
SKETCHES OF MOUNTAIN MEMORIES

October, 1992

To Fiona and Mike,
With love.
Merry Christmas!
Joe and Milli

Bright Mountain Books
Asheville, North Carolina

Cover and text illustrations by Carol Schell Bruckner

Printed in the United States of America
ISBN: 0-914875-20-5

Library of Congress Cataloging-in-Publication Data

Morgan, Joe Richard, 1934–
    Potato Branch : sketches of mountain memories / Joe Richard Morgan.
        p.   cm.
    ISBN 0-914875-20-5.
    1. Blue Ridge Mountains—Social life and customs. 2. Morgan, Joe Richard, 1934– —Childhood and youth. 3. Blue Ridge Mountains—Biography. I. Title.
    F262.B6M67   1992
    975.5'043—dc20   92-24274
                                                                          CIP

In memory of
Mother and Dad

ACKNOWLEDGEMENTS

I acknowledge the kindnesses of the many who have read these stories and made suggestions for making each line carry the freight I intended. Especially I thank Ellen Hoffman, my neighbor and a writer; Elaine Derk, my secretary; Cynthia Bright, my editor; and Milli Way, my wife, for their keen observations, careful readings, and constructive criticism.

CONTENTS

NEIGHBOR

LOVER

MARINE

The Stories I Always Intended to Write

I wrote *Potato Branch* because of a compulsion to make some record of a fascinating era in American country life or, to be more precise, an era in Appalachian mountain life. I wanted to tell people what it was like to grow up in the Blue Ridge Mountains of the 1930s and 1940s. I wanted to introduce the world to the unique people who lived in the small valley in which I was born. That valley is known today as Morgan Branch.

This compulsion, however, took a long time to assume any practical form. I seemed to winnow it by telling my wife and my children about happenings in my youth. Those were the years before, during, and after World War II—the years of Edward R. Murrow and Kate Smith and "Our Gal Sunday" on the radio; of President Roosevelt's fireside chats and Sir Winston Churchill's speeches and the reports from abroad coming and fading on the short-wave radio; of following the teams of mules in the fields; of going to the "movies" on Saturday nights in Dad's Model-A Ford. We sped along the gravel road toward Asheville at twenty-five miles per hour, maybe up to thirty down the hills.

I began life in a tradition or culture that is now foreign to many other Americans. The wonderful old folks who live in these stories have long since departed this earth except for the markers on their graves in scattered cemeteries. All names are real and accurate, but I have taken the liberty of combining some events, because thereby I could be more economical with time and space. My relationship to my family and neighbors is outlined on page 164.

It was my mother's letters to me when I was away in the United States Marine Corps during the Korean War that planted the seeds of some of the stories I would write. One was the story I titled "Marshall Gregg." "No one will ever believe what he did because real life is stranger than fiction," she wrote. Of course, Mother gave me the challenge. The world ought to know how two men loved the same woman and how that woman came to settle their life-long loves when they aged into their eighties. I told it as a mystery story because much of Marshall's life was a mystery to me.

After I had taught literature and writing for many years, I began to write stories to show my students how a story is shaped, how to develop character, how to focus on a theme and leave the reader to make of the truth whatever he would. As I wrote, I did not put down my memories in a chronological order; rather I wrote as one event or person reminded me of an earlier or later one. I believe the arrangement here presents the stories in a logical order. The stories are grouped by my relationship to the people about whom I write. Within each group the order is mostly chronological.

I have no reason to live in the past, as I am still a practicing teacher, still enjoying life, still learning from my students and neighbors. But to me, my past is a sweet, safe place and I like to spend a little time there now and then.

Potato Branch

BOY

The Clodbuster

"Whoa!" my father shouted to the mules and jerked the reins. Tom and Kate stopped. Dad held the reins taut. He had been walking behind the heavy clodbuster while my twin sisters and I rode in the large trays on top. The machine frame held a row of heavy, iron rollers that crushed clods.

I was six. The twins, two years younger than I, were with Dad and me in the field because Mother was in the hospital again. We had been riding back and forth, climbing higher up the hillside with each turn. Progress over the clods came in jerks and jolts as the team labored to pull the heavy, pointed rollers over the rough, hard clay. We laughed as the machine rode upon large clods of earth and then dropped with a bump when the clods burst beneath us.

Suddenly, in a jolt, my sister, Dot, who was on the downhill end of the machine, was pitched forward. She tumbled face down between the mule's singletree and the heavy rollers. When the team stopped, she lay with her hands stretched forward near Kate's heels and her legs pinned under the clodbuster.

I looked down at Dot and then back at Dad. For a moment he stood immobile, his face pale. Then he said, "Joe, son, climb down."

I jumped off the clodbuster and stood beside him. I felt his hand tremble as he handed me the reins. "Hold them tight," he told me.

He lifted Dean off the crusher and stood her like a doll on the ground near me. We were quiet and we stood still. I could see the bottoms of Dot's bare feet pressed in the recesses between the sharp ridges of the rollers. She was quiet too.

Dad couldn't back the roller off her because one mule would step on her. Nor, of course, could he risk a stir which would cause the team to roll the clodbuster forward. She lay pinned at the heels of Kate, a nervous, jumpy animal.

As my father stepped around the clodbuster, he spoke softly to the team. "Whoa, Tom. Hold still. Be still, Kate," he said, patting her on the rump.

"Sister," he said to Dot, "I'll get you out in a minute." As he patted Kate with one hand, he cupped his left hand over the end of her singletree. Then he unhooked her right trace, and the other one in turn. He left Kate's collar attached to the tongue. Tom stood still, taking a brief rest. It was Kate who would be likely to stomp her feet in her harness. He didn't bother with Tom's traces.

Next, Dad stepped to the end of the clodbuster and took hold of the frame. Then he said, "Dot, when I lift it up, you crawl out between the mule's heels and the rollers. Be quick."

To me he said, "Joe, don't let Kate turn her head. She might think Dot is a dog and kick her."

I held the reins and watched the mules' heads. Dad lifted the end of the clodbuster and Dot crawled out to safety.

4

As I grew older and stronger and passed the heavy clodbuster in the machine shed, I often stopped and tried to lift one end. I never ever raised it a millimeter.

Beehives and Outhouses

Midway across the footbridge spanning the mountain creek I stopped. I grasped the handrail and gazed at the four beehives that stood along the bank of a smaller stream just where it joined the big creek. Three large plum trees sheltered the hives. The hum in the beehives was louder than usual, and clusters of bees boiled out of one hive.

I had thought I would be the last one to use the old, three-seater outhouse that stood over the little branch near the hives, but I was not.

Works Project Administration men had been busy for two days building a new single-seat outhouse that would have a cement floor, a shaped wooden seat with a lid, and be placed over a deep pit at the corner of the cherry orchard. It would be treated with black creosote and stand boldly in the open.

It had none of the romance or adventure of the old whitewashed outhouse perched precariously over the stream near the beehives. Three giant lilac bushes that shielded the old house perfumed the air in April and drew the bees and hummingbirds in their hunt for nectar.

A well-worn path led between two tall lilac bushes, then diverged in the grass toward two doors located at each end of the wide white house. Inside, the long bench seat displayed three perfectly round holes that opened clear down to the cold, rushing stream below. A broom stood in one corner behind the door, a magazine rack hung on the center wall, and a Sears, Roebuck catalog lay on the bench. While one sat, he could wrinkle a page of slick, colorful copy into a soft, rag-like tissue. Single bees from the hives were known to buzz many a bare bottom there.

Instead of going into the old outhouse, I rushed back across the bridge to Aunt Bess's kitchen. "Aunt Bess, the bees are mad!" I shouted as the screen door slammed behind me.

Aunt Bess laughed and asked, "How do you know?"

"Just you come and see," I begged.

By then the air outside hummed with hosts of bees buzzing in every direction away from the plum grove.

"We must settle the bees," Aunt Bess told me as we went back into the kitchen.

"Why are they leaving?" I asked.

"They're swarming," she answered.

"Why are they swarming?"

"There may be two queens in that hive or ants may have invaded their honey. Your dad will find out. Better get the bell."

It became my job to settle the bees when they swarmed. Aunt Bess reached for the old family school bell in the corner cupboard where she kept it. It was the schoolmaster's bell from the time Grandfather had the teacher living there and holding classes in the south wing of the house. It was a hand bell of good size with a clear tone.

I went out on the lawn ringing the bell constantly. The *clang, clang, clang* would cause the bees to settle quickly. Dad told me later that ringing interferes with the high-pitched noise the queen emits to keep the bees together. She settles to regain her bearings.

Of course, the crew of W.P.A. outhouse carpenters were aware of the commotion. One man said, "It's our hammering that's stirred 'em up."

Dad said, "Oh, no, just keep working, it'll help settle 'em. I'll ready a new gum." All mountain people use both terms *hive* and *gum* to mean where the bees are kept. In the wild, bees use a hollow gum tree for their hive.

Another man came toward the house and told Aunt Bess he was afraid of getting stung. She declared, "They won't sting now. And, besides, bee stings are good for arthritis."

"Nevertheless, I don't care for that kind of medicine," he replied.

"Keep ringing the bell," Aunt Bess told me as she went back into the kitchen. She returned with a tin dishpan which she beat with a wooden spoon.

The W.P.A. carpenters worked on to finish the new outhouse while Dad went to the granary where Grandfather kept several clean homemade gums made of wood planks. "A swarm of bees in May is worth a stack of hay," he declared as he brought a spare plank gum into the yard to ready it for the bees. "These bees will make sourwood honey if we can settle them into a new gum."

I kept ringing the bell as I watched Dad ready the gum for a colony of bees. He brushed it out. Then he walked to the little volunteer peach tree near the old can house and cut off a limb covered with leaves. Aunt Bess brought him some honey water which he poured over the leaves. With the limb he sprinkled the inside of the new gum.

Meanwhile the bees began to settle on a low limb of a juniper bush that grew at the edge of the lawn near the barn lot fence. The new queen had landed there first and she was followed there by her drones and her workers. Thousands of bees tried to occupy the same space around their queen. Soon the entire colony clung in a cluster around the ever-green limb. They looked like a large, living football as the juniper limb sagged with their weight.

I had learned some things about bees at school. Our teacher, Miss Cole, had a glass hive in a classroom window. We could watch the bees while they worked in the hive. Screens on the windows kept bees from entering the class-room.

Often at recess I had stood watching those bees in the glass hive. Once Miss Cole explained to several of us how a German professor had studied honey bees for forty years and had discovered how to read bee language.

I watched worker bees do their "round dance." A bee would whirl in a circle turning left and right for just a few seconds. Other bees clustered around the "dancer," then left the hive. The dance told the other bees where the nectar could be found. The round dance indicated that the source of the nectar would be found in a radius of about four hundred feet of the hive.

A honey bee gave more elaborate directions to his fellow workers by a "wagging dance." The bee would run in a semicircle, then straight back to its starting position. Then the dancer would perform another semicircle in the opposite direction. The bee would repeat the performance for several minutes. Somehow this dance also told the direction of the nectar and the distance it was away from the hive. I loved to watch the bees and try to read their language.

"Stop ringing that bell!" I heard Dad shout. Holding the bell by its clapper, I ventured closer to watch Dad get the settled swarm into its new home. A few guard bees still buzzed around the colony.

Dad spread a sheet on the lawn near the juniper, set the empty hive on it, and sprinkled the opening at the bottom with honey water from the peach limb.

Uncle Taylor brought Dad some gloves and a hand saw. Just as he waded carefully into the juniper bush, one of the guard bees settled on my wrist and I slapped at it. It stung me and left its stinger in the spot.

"Ouch!" I said, "I'm stung."

Dad turned to me, removed his gloves, and pulled out the stinger. "That bee will die without his stinger," he said, and added, "You ought not to have slapped at him. Stand still if you're going to watch."

He spit some tobacco juice on the sting and told me to pull a plantain leaf and rub it on the spot. "That'll take care of it," he said and went back to the juniper bush.

Uncle Taylor held the tip of the juniper limb as Dad sawed it off the tree. Together, they carried it to the gum where they sprinkled the bees with honey water and then shook the bees from the limb onto the sheet in front of the hive. Ever so slowly the bees began to crawl into their new home.

By the time Dad and Uncle Taylor had taken care of the bees, the W.P.A. crew had finished the new outhouse, stained it with creosote, gathered their tools, and driven away in their truck.

Later, I stood on the footbridge to watch Dad and Uncle Taylor place the new beegum on the rack beside the other hives under the plum trees.

Suddenly, remembering, I ran off across the bridge toward the cherry orchard to be the first in the new single-seat outhouse.

Grandfather Morgan

My cousin Ruth Anne and I sat on the linoleum rug in the light of a tall window playing Monopoly and keeping Grandfather company while Aunt Bess "ran" to the garden and the hen house and the smoke house and the well house and got dinner ready in the kitchen. Grandfather lay quietly, a tube from him draining into a glass jar on the floor beside the bed.

The room smelled of medicine and tobacco and bedpan and Pinesol.

It was my turn as Monopoly banker, but Ruth Anne had all the railroads, Boardwalk and Park Place with hotels, plus other streets of real estate. It was only a matter of time before Chance would land me into bankruptcy.

We played quietly so not to disturb Grandfather. When he needed anything, one of us ran for Aunt Bess.

Grandfather kept his walking cane beside him, lying on the bedsheet next to the wall. He often forgot we were there near him, and he would pick up his stick and tap the wall, a signal for Aunt Bess to come from the kitchen.

The walls in his bedroom were panelled in hand-hewn chestnut. I remember one wide board, perhaps eighteen inches wide, that Grandfather kept hitting with his cane. It was leaving marks in the soft, varnished chestnut.

Suddenly, as Ruth Anne and I played Monopoly, Grandfather began striking the wall with his cane.

"Grandpa, we're here," I said as I jumped up beside him.

"Bessie!" he called, and he kept tapping the wall. Aunt Bess stepped through the doorway from the dining hall and appeared at the foot of his bed.

"Papa," she said gently, "you're scarring up this whole wall with that cane."

"I hewed that wall, Bessie," he retorted weakly, "and if I want to hit it, I'll hit it."

Aunt Bess lifted his head, fluffed up his pillows, gave him some water and medicine, then sat on the bedside and talked with him a bit. When she got up to go, she looked at the scarred panelling and then at Grandfather whose eyes were following her. Aunt Bess smiled as she said, "Yes, Papa, you've got more right than anyone to hit this wall, so don't mind me. Just tap it when you need me."

"Thanks, Bess," he sighed and closed his eyes.

*   *   *

I remember Grandfather as a remarkable old man. Dad told me that on the day I was born, Grandfather and Uncle Ernest were hauling logs to the sawmill. On a return trip with the mules and wagon they drove by the house, and Dr. Pilgrim went out and called, "Mr. Morgan, come in here and see your new grandson." I was named after my two grandfathers, Joe Anders and Richard Cansler Morgan.

Grandfather was known as "Uncle Canse" throughout Newfound Valley. Deacon of Zion Hill Baptist Church, a highway commissioner of Buncombe County, and landowner, he was a respected citizen. Once the only Morgan on Newfound, he had bought land on Potato Branch, married

Martha Cole, fathered thirteen children, built a large home, and lived to hear Potato Branch called Morgan Branch.

He always stood or sat "ram-rod straight" as Mother would say. His old T-Model truck also stood tall and straight in the cow shed where I often went to play. I would sit in its high seat, hold the large steering wheel, and look out over the short hood from his driver's seat.

When Grandfather drove the "T" into our yard, Mother would hold me by the hand. "Don't get near that truck," she would say.

The Model-T had three pedals on the floorboard: a brake pedal, a forward gear pedal, and a reverse pedal. When Grandfather decided to back the truck out of the yard into the road, he simply pressed the reverse pedal and steered backwards, never turning his head to look behind him. He sat erect, looking straight ahead through the top half of the two-panelled windscreen. Everyone knew better than to stand behind Grandfather's truck when he was in the driver's seat.

Grandfather had style. Mother told me of the time she and Dad were riding with him from Asheville. A young highway patrolman hailed them and explained that he was inspecting cars for safety.

The patrolman stood on the running board and instructed Grandfather to "just do as I tell you." He rode a small piece and shouted, "Stop!" As usual, Grandfather hit the reverse pedal, a drive wheel spun backwards, and they stopped.

"You don't have any brakes!" the officer exclaimed.

Sitting erect and still in the high seat, Grandfather said

14

with an air of polite command, "I stopped, sir. You said 'stop' and I stopped. There's no trouble here. Now, young man, step off and get ready to inspect the next car. You're doing your job just fine."

The patrolman, speechless, stepped down onto the gravel. Grandfather pressed the forward pedal. The epicyclic train of gears in the planetary transmission grabbed, and the old Model-T lurched toward home.

* * *

A few mornings later as Ruth Anne and I were quietly playing a game of Chinese Checkers, we listened to Grandfather's slow and painful breathing. Aunt Bess came into the bedroom, looked Grandfather over, checked his catheter, and slipped her hand under the bedsheet to feel his feet.

"Papa, your feet are cold!" she said.

He opened his eyes. "It won't be long now, Bessie," he whispered. "I don't feel them."

Aunt Bess uncovered and looked at his feet. They were turning blue.

"Joe Dicky," she told me, "find your daddy and tell him to come here quickly."

Dad and Uncle Taylor stood at the foot of his bed. Aunt Bess sat on the bed next to the wall and held Grandfather's hand while Doctor Reeves knelt on the window side, listening to Grandfather's heartbeat with his stethoscope. Ruth Anne and I listened to the death rattle in Grandpa's throat.

Grandpa muttered something, but Aunt Bess, tears streaming down her face, said, "I didn't understand it."

Then Grandfather was gone.

15

Winter Foxes

Mother treadled the sewing machine in sudden bursts as she stitched the garment together. She had cut the pattern on material from print feed sacks she had saved and washed for the twins' new dresses.

The wind outside whistled and whined around the house. Gusts rattled the tin roof. Dad pulled back the curtain and peered into the growing darkness, then he turned to Mother. "Della," he asked, "did you shut the hen house door? That fox will come back tonight."

"Yes," she answered. "I went back after they all went to roost. Didn't expect them to go in after last night, but I fed them in front of the house and threw some corn meal inside."

"Looks like it'll snow tonight, and if it does we can track him back to his den tomorrow. It'd be a good time to have a fox hound," Dad mused.

"I think it's a vixen the way she tore under the house and took the hen with her. She probably wanted food for her kits."

"Well, I put a big rock against that loose board," Dad added. "It can't get in that way again."

While we sat before a blazing fire, an occasional down draft sent smoke curling out of the fireplace. The flame in the kerosene lamp beside Mother's machine flickered. When the wind howled, the blue patterned linoleum rug on the

living room floor rose like a magic carpet trying to break free
of the furniture that held it down. In those days we had
only a subfloor between us and the earth beneath.

The butter churn, the hearth oven, and clothes iron
stood close to the fire dogs. We'd had cornbread and butter-
milk for supper. Mother reached often for the iron to press
a seam as she sewed.

Above our heads, hanging from permanent hooks in the
ceiling, was a quilting frame with a partly finished quilt
stretched on it. Mother lowered the frame and quilted when
no one was using the living room. It was now drawn up
near the ceiling.

Dad had read us the evening Bible story, but it was still
too early for bed. Dean stood by the machine watching
Mother work. Dot paged through one of Mother's "True
Stories" magazines, and I begged Dad to play checkers with
me, but he said "not tonight." From time to time he held
the curtain back and peered out into the darkness.

"How would you children like to catch a fox?" Mother
asked as she kept working. Dad watched her hands as
Mother guided the cloth under the flashing needle and
treadled the machine into a trembling roar.

"What do you mean?" Dean asked while Mother turned
the material. She lowered the presser foot and needle and
then turned to us as we stood beside her machine.

"It's something your Grandfather Anders showed me
a long time ago. We'll need a few things you all can collect."

To me she said, "Put your coat on, go to the barn, and
bring us one big ear of white corn." While I got my coat
and Dad lit the lantern for me, Mother asked Dean to get

17

her a pencil and a ruler. Dot must have gone for cardboard, because when I returned with the ear of corn Dad was helping Dot cut a piece from the side of a box.

"What's that?" I asked.

"It will be a game board," Dad explained.

Mother laid the new dress on the machine leaf. Next, she placed the cardboard on the linoleum rug and drew a playing field. It contained five equal squares that together formed a cross. Inside each square she drew four lines that intersected in the center, and then she drew a circle at each corner and at each intersection and wrote letters near some of them.

Mother told me, "Shell some large grains of corn from that ear and I'll show you how to play Fox and Geese. Each grain of corn will represent one goose. We'll need twenty-two geese."

"What's the fox?" Dot asked.

Mother turned to her sewing basket. "Here are two thimbles for the foxes." She handed them to Dot.

"Wouldn't you say *foxen* since you have more than one?" Dad teased. "We call more than one ox *oxen*."

"It's *foxes* when you have two," Mother said to us. "Don't confuse them, Buddy," she added for Dad.

Then she said, "Dot, put your foxes here," and she indicated points B and C on the board. "That end of the board belongs to the foxes but they may not move down into it."

I had shelled enough corn. "Now put one goose on each circle except on these two at the corners," said Mother as she pointed to points A and D on the board. "Don't put any geese behind the foxes."

When the pieces were in place, Mother explained, "The object of the game for the foxes is to capture the geese. Either fox can move once per move. A fox can capture a goose when he jumps over a goose into an empty space. The object of the game for the geese players is to corner the foxes so they can't move at all. Since both foxes can be in one space at one time it means it's better to corner them separately. See! A fox can jump or move into a space occupied by the other fox. That's why they are so tricky to corner. The geese may move along a line into any empty space, but they may not jump a fox or another goose or an empty space."

"Can a goose move behind the foxes?" I asked.

"No, that line is called the fence." Mother pointed to the line between points B and C. "I'll play the first game with you to show you how. I'll be the foxes," Mother announced, "and a fox always makes the first move." Dot, Dean, and I became the geese.

Soon the geese were captured. As Dad, Dot, Dean, or I took our turn at playing the foxes, we hardly noticed the winter wind or Mother's treadle sending her needle singing along the seams of the second dress.

NEPHEW

Santa Claus

"'Twas the night before Christmas," my father read to me and my sisters, "when all through the house, not a creature was stirring, not even a mouse." We were piled on his lap in his chair by the window, me on one leg and the twins on the other. In my pajamas I curled into his chest with my thumb in my mouth and closed my eyes to listen.

The open fire blazed warm below three, long, red stockings Mother had helped us hang on the mantelpiece. We expected an orange and an apple and some peppermints in each stocking on Christmas morning. Mother had washed up our supper dishes, replaced the hearth oven, and had sat down in her chair near us in front of the fire. She picked up her sewing.

Somewhere deep in the story, A Visit from St. Nicholas, I heard harness bells jingling and the snorting of mules, a clatter rising on our lawn right outside the window where we sat in Dad's rocking chair. I started to jump down, but Dad held me tightly and said, "We've not finished our story."

"Don't you hear somethin'?" I asked.

Mother smiled and said, "It must be Santa Claus coming early tonight." We listened as we heard Santa shout "Whoa!"

We sat very still. My sister, Dean, began to cry.

"Can we see the reindeer?" I begged as I stretched

toward the window to reach the curtain.

But Dad held me fast and said, "No! You would scare Santa's reindeer. Be still and listen."

"He come down chimney?" my sister Dot asked. The fire burned hot in the fireplace.

"Santa comes down the chimney only when he can't get through the door," Dad explained. There were three steps on the porch and then a loud rap at the kitchen door. Mother rose to answer it.

From Dad's lap I heard Mother say, "Oh, Santa, come in! The children are on their daddy's lap." He tromped through the kitchen and stood a moment in the doorway to the living room.

"Ho! Ho! Ho!" he laughed. He was the exact picture of St. Nicholas of our storybook. Above his black boots, his red outfit was trimmed in white fur. His ample, round belly shook when he laughed. He wore a wide black belt with the large brass buckle on his tummy. His red cap came down over his ears. His long, white beard was "white as the snow."

When he stepped into the room, we saw a full white sack on his back. He came over in front of the fire and stood on the hearth, set his pack on the rug, and asked us our names. I told him "Joe" with my thumb in my mouth. Dot just looked at him with her thumb in her mouth. Dean said, "She's my sister."

Then Santa Claus noticed our Christmas tree that stood almost behind Dad's rocker. Mother had helped us string popcorn which was wrapped around the tree, and she had made colored paper rings and looped them chain-like and

24

wrapped those on the tree. Mother had also tied popcorn balls on the tree. Santa asked us if we had decorated the tree. When we said yes, Dad said, "You better tell Santa that your mother did most of the work."

"It's a very nice tree, Della," Santa said, and I noticed that Aunt Ruth and Aunt Bess had come in too. They stood beside Mother watching us. Aunt Bess smiled from ear to ear. It didn't occur to me then that Uncle Lloyd and Uncle Taylor were missing.

To me Santa turned first and asked, "Have you been a good boy?"

"Oh, yes!" I said and put my thumb back into my mouth.

"All year?" he asked.

"Yep," I muttered.

"I see you suck your thumb," he said with a wrinkled brow.

I took it out of my mouth.

Santa reached out and took my hand. He looked at my thumb and laughed his "Ho! Ho! Ho!" Then he said, "Well, I can't give any toys to a boy that sucks his thumb."

All were very quiet. My heart pounded in my chest. A tear rolled down my cheek. Then Santa said, "Maybe if you promise not to suck your thumb for a whole year, I could give you some toys this year."

I said I'd promise, and I stuck my thumb back into my mouth. Then I jerked it out again, but Santa had noticed.

He reached for my thumb again and held my hand firmly. He turned to Mother and said, "The only cure I can think of is to cut it off. Please get me a butcher knife."

Mother brought the knife and Santa took it in his free hand. He held it near my knuckle and studied where to cut. I shook with dread. I couldn't speak. Then I heard Aunt Ruth whisper, "Lloyd!" or "Lord!"; I couldn't tell which. Then she said, "Santa, don't scare the children to death!"

Aunt Bess said, "Santa, I think if Joe promises not to suck his thumb, then he can have his presents. It's not easy to break a habit."

"OK," Santa said, "but if you don't stop for a year then I won't bring you any presents next Christmas."

He opened his pack and gave us presents. Dot and Dean got dolls that wet their diapers, and I got some matchbox cars. Later, Santa went back to his sled and brought us a little red wagon which he said Uncle Ernest had given to him to give to us.

He had presents in his sack for Mother and Dad too, and he handed out the gifts from under our Christmas tree. He took some cookies that Mother had baked for him and a glass of eggnog. Aunt Ruth and Aunt Bess took some cookies too.

"Well, I must get on my way," Santa said as he picked up his empty sack. "Merry Christmas to all, and to all a good night!"

Again Dot, Dean, and I wanted to see his reindeer but were not permitted to look. We could hear Santa laughing outside. He pecked on the window pane and waved good-bye.

Soon we heard Santa shout, "Now, Dasher! Now, Dancer! Now, Prancer and Vixen! On, Comet! On, Cupid! On, Donder and Blitzen! To the top of the porch, to the top of the wall! Now, dash away! Dash away! Dash away all!"

It was a dark, cold night with just a dusting of snow and frost. I heard harness bells jingle and a sled dragged into the gravel road that led toward Uncle Taylor's barn, and above it all, a great, deep laughter from Santa.

On Christmas morning we found our stockings stuffed with an orange, an apple, some nuts, and a popcorn ball. We had the orange with our breakfast oatmeal. Dad said that Santa must have remembered them later and come back.

When Dad went to milk the cows, I went to look for the tracks of Santa's sled and reindeer. They were there. The tracks were wide ones. They came across our yard and led into the road toward Uncle Taylor's barn. When Mother came out to go to the barn, I said, "These hoof prints look like mule shoes to me."

Mother said, "They are reindeer tracks. You've just never seen reindeer tracks before."

I followed the tracks out under the white pine that stood by the road and saw a new, little, red matchbox fire engine lying in the frosty grass. "Look at this, Mom," I yelled.

"Santa must have dropped it last night," she said. "I'm sure he meant it for you."

*   *   *

Later that spring when everyone was doing house cleaning and I was helping Aunt Bess at her house, Ruth Anne, my cousin, whispered that she had something to show me.

We went into a guest room where Uncle Lloyd and Aunt Ruth spent the weekends and the Christmas holidays.

Ruth Anne pulled out the bottom drawer of the dresser, and there was a red Santa Claus outfit trimmed in white fur. We didn't touch it, just closed the drawer and got back downstairs before Aunt Bess learned we were snooping, but I knew then that I couldn't risk sucking my thumb anymore. I was afraid the song was right.

Aunt Bess

"Bud found a young man to preach the revival next week," Uncle Taylor told Aunt Bess as we watched the installation men carrying the crane-like, aluminum aerial over the yard. The long line attached to the aerial led to the new black and white television set in the corner of the kitchen. Searching for the best place to erect the antenna, the men long considered placing it on a post in the tobacco patch. Finally it was mounted high above one of the chimneys. The mountains made television reception a tricky science, and another antenna of tubes that curved like twin trombones was placed low on a post in the yard to receive the Greenville TV signals that bounced off Mount Pisgah. "Did Bud say who the evangelist is this year?" Aunt Bess asked Uncle Taylor.

"A young preacher from Beaver Dam. He's not heard him preach, but the folks on Pole Creek said he was a fireball."

Uncle Bud Mehaffey, as everyone called him, was married to my Aunt Estelle, another of Dad's sisters. He had pastored Zion Hill Baptist Church for many years, and he always chose the revival preacher. As the week passed I heard snatches of talk between Uncle Taylor and Aunt Bess on the topic of revivals past and the one to come.

"Remember how Preacher Mann railed against reading the cartoons and the Sunday funnies?" Aunt Bess asked while she was milking Jersey Bell.

"And women's magazines too, I think," Uncle Taylor answered. "You didn't stop your subscriptions though."

"They horse fly!" Aunt Bess exclaimed.

Their talk of Preacher Mann made my skin prickle a bit with my own memory. After one of his sermons, I would not get the Sunday funnies until after dinner when I would take the papers to the porch swing, sit and browse them. I never confessed this to any person. God Himself was taking his afternoon nap.

When Buttercup and Jersey Bell were turned into the barn lot after milking, Uncle Taylor carried the milk to the house. I went with Aunt Bess to feed the chickens. They gathered close around her feet. One rooster pecked at her legs. She flapped her apron at him and said, "You tough old bird, I'll boil you in dumplin's and feed you to the preacher on Sunday."

The preacher on Sunday was Uncle Bud. "The Righteous shall flourish like the Palm Tree," he declared, developing an image of the palm tree that grows on sandy beaches, bends with the wind, brings forth its fruit in its season like the godly man of Psalm 1.

After church, Uncle Bud and Aunt Estelle came to Uncle Taylor and Aunt Bessie's for dinner. Uncle Lloyd and Aunt Ruth Plemmons were there and my family too.

While the women prepared the table, the men sat in the shade under the mimosa trees and talked. Uncle Lloyd smoked his pipe, the fragrance of Prince Albert tobacco mingling with the mimosa blossoms.

Uncle Bud told stories on himself. Once after a Sunday

meeting, he was invited to eat dinner with a farm family back in the hills. When he sat down at their table, he noticed a small bowl of peaches beside his plate. There were at least six small children around the table with their parents. They talked and ate and Uncle Bud picked up the bowl of peaches and put it on his plate and ate the peaches as his dessert.

"I wondered why those big brown eyes watched me so intently as I finished eating," he told. "It was then I saw that no one else had a bowl of peaches beside his plate. I had eaten all the family dessert."

Uncle Lloyd laughed with him and asked, "What did you do?"

"Took 'em a bushel of peaches the next Sunday. You should have seen those children's eyes when I set the basket on the porch."

Everyone laughed.

Aunt Bess called, "Dinner!"

My job at the table was to keep the flies away while the first tableful ate their meal. Grandmother Morgan had a straight sassafras stick with a thick row of brown paper ribbons cut from grocery bags fastened to the end. I waved the fly scare over the heads of the diners when I saw a fly dive for any dish on the table. Otherwise, I was to be seen and not heard.

I listened. They talked of the weather and the tobacco and the corn and the potatoes and the revival to start that evening.

"We need someone who will teach the Bible," Aunt Bess put in. "We don't need him to rail against some sin.

We've heard enough about tobacco and liquor."

"It'd do Lloyd good," Aunt Ruth said, "He smokes too much. Eating, though, is his besetting sin. Just look at that stomach." Uncle Lloyd laughed and patted his round middle.

Sometimes Uncle Taylor had a beer or two after a day in the hot Morgan Furniture Factory. I knew that some people thought beer his besetting sin, and I knew that Aunt Bess did not want him offended. Besides, there was the tobacco patch just outside the yard, Uncle Taylor's money crop.

Uncle Bud, keen on the uptake, as Dad would say, told another story.

"After my first heart attack, Bessie, my doctor told me that I needed building up. He gave me this expensive prescription. I asked him, 'Isn't there some other way to build me up?' And he told me, 'Yes, you could get the same thing from a bottle of malt beer each day, but your being a preacher and all that . . .'

"Well, the short of it is that I got me a case of beer and I drink a bottle with my supper each day. Makes me sleep, don't it, Estelle?"

Aunt Estelle was a teetotaler. "I reckon it's all right if the doctor says so," she said. "As long as one don't get to liking it."

"How can you like it?" Aunt Ruth asked. "It looks and tastes like horse piss and foams like it too." Everyone laughed.

"What's your besetting sin, Bessie?" Uncle Bud asked. "It can't be gluttony, you haven't sat down for a full minute this whole meal."

"It's work," Uncle Taylor answered for her. "We ought to take a vacation, but she won't go."

"You can't leave a farm," Aunt Bess argued. "The cows've got to be milked and the chickens fed, holiday or not."

Everyone knew the truth of that. As she picked up a plate and started for the dishpan, she added, "I'll take my vacation in heaven."

Uncle Taylor said, "Me and Bess watch TV most every night now. It's kinda like a vacation."

At church that evening, the young, new preacher, looking full of holy mission, sat in the ornate chair on the speaker's platform and watched the congregation during the first part of the service.

The choir sang:
Revive us again. Fill each heart with Thy love.
May each soul be rekindled with fire from above.
Hallelujah! Thine the glory. Hallelujah, Amen.
Hallelujah! Thine the glory. REE-VIVE US AGAIN.

Peering through her bifocals at the sheet music, Mrs. Pearl Robertson played the piano while her daughter, Martha, sang "I Won't Have to Cross Jordan Alone."

The offering was taken.

At last Uncle Bud introduced the new preacher. Aunt Bess and Uncle Taylor sat together on a long pew. They looked intently and expectantly toward the young man.

He stepped to the podium, youthful, roughly handsome with a cowlick of hair that stood up like a cock's comb. He looked over the audience of patient, work-weary mountain people, everyone intent on hearing him. It was a dramatic moment.

"THE DEVIL'S GOT THIS COMMUNITY," he announced. Then with a kind of flashing, wild-eyed look, he continued, "I seen his horns on the houses as I drove down the valley . . . ."

It must have been Aunt Bess who first realized that *horns* meant television antennae. She bowed her head and chuckled quietly. Uncle Taylor whispered "Sh-h-h," as he kept his composure. Aunt Bess bit her lip and grabbed her sides and she began to shake. The pew shook with her, and faces, stern and sober, bent forward and glared at her while the preacher's voice grew in intensity.

"Bess, be quiet," Uncle Taylor whispered. His melancholy face and solemn attitude destroyed all hopes of mastering her convulsions. Then someone on the pew gave an impatient "Sh-h-h!" She began to wipe tears from her eyes and Uncle Taylor said quietly, "Bess, if you can't sit still, we'll have to leave."

Aunt Bess got up suddenly and hurried to the back of the church and on outside. Then Uncle Taylor, with his head bowed, tiptoed down the aisle behind her, his gray felt hat held at his side.

I knew they went home to laugh and to watch TV.

Bull Fight

As spring fence mending came to an end, it was Uncle R. D. who declared, "They's no bull going through that fence!" He and Uncle Oliver and Mr. Mark Daves had stretched two more strands of new barbed-wire on the old ridge fence, making eight strands fastened to locust posts which stood at four-foot intervals. It was a formidable fence that ran the line between Uncle Oliver's and Mr. Mark's mountain pastures.

The next day both cattlemen turned out their prize beef cattle from the winter lots onto the high pastures.

Uncle Oliver had the larger herd of purebred Herefords with a new, fully grown, registered whiteface bull that weighed over 1800 pounds. Mr. Mark had a small herd of Herefords too. His bull, which serviced his heifers, was younger and about 300 pounds lighter than Uncle Oliver's whiteface.

From our front yard across the bottomland corn I had a clear view of Mr. Mark's side of the mountain pasture. The strong line fence ran the ridge from the Daves mountain on the left to the timbered knoll on the right that dropped off into the high fields of Uncle Oliver's farm.

On a summer's evening one could often see a bull stride across the landscape and hear him bellow as he lumbered toward some tree trunk which he would rub against to scratch himself.

But in the early afternoon on that spring day Uncle Oliver's whiteface bull walked the line fence and bellowed a challenge to Mr. Mark's redhead bull that grazed with his cows on the hillside below. Tommy, Mr. Mark's bull, looked up the hill at the large whiteface and bellowed back. Then he pawed the ground as he took a few lunges up toward the fence. He threw turfs of grass behind him and bellowed from the depth of his strong lungs. His will to fight showed in the switch of his tail, the stomp of his hind hoofs, and the tossing of his head.

Uncle Oliver's whiteface pawed the ground too and threw turfs of sod behind him with his fore hoofs. He fell on his knees and bellowed low and loudly and long. Then he raced along the fence as if to find a way around it.

Tommy bellowed louder and climbed nearer to the fence, pawing sod and advancing with his head lowered. Both bulls pawed and paced their respective sides of the fence bellowing in a duet that rumbled from some deep inferno.

The whiteface charged the fence. He walked on his hind legs and crashed down on it. He reared up and raised the volume of his bellow to a menacing roar. Tommy, too, lunged at the whiteface against the fence and bounced back from the eight strands of tight wire.

Mr. Mark's cows, which had stood mute watching, turned in a trot and scattered to the shade of trees on the opposite hillside.

Uncle R. D. and Aunt Ruby heard the bulls' bellow and drove down to our house to see what was happening. Others stopped farm work and found a clear view at a respectful distance. For many, the view was from their truck bed parked along the road near our house. The thunder of bull bellows rumbled in the valley.

Suddenly the fence gave way before the combined weight and ferocity of the two animals. Locust posts broke and barbed-wire hurled into tangles as the two bulls rode down the fence and locked heads in their duel.

Both had been dehorned when quite young so that the fight was to go to strength and weight rather than to a lucky gore with horns. The fighters tore up the sod in a streak down Mr. Mark's pasture as they butted and bellowed and hurled themselves at each other. No one mentioned separating them. Spectators stood speechless. All could tell that some primeval struggle had begun, some ancient rite, some mysterious survival of the fittest was taking place. The cattle breeders stood silent too. Dad passed his binoculars to me and I took a closer gaze.

At first, in each attack the bulls locked heads, pawing the earth, and then fell to their fore knees. They held their tails high in a twist above their stretched hind legs while the great scrotums swung near the ground. Each grappled for footholds in his desperate struggle. This was no scuffle of steers for room at the manger.

The snorting grew in intensity along with the deep, bass bellows. As the battle ebbed and flowed as first one bull, then the other, backed his adversary back and forth across the hill in the long afternoon, it seemed that each bull's capacity for taking falls and side thrusts was endless. A streak of green hillside slowly turned to clay under the stomping, churning feet.

A bull kills by goring and falling on his victim, and this instinctive knowledge kept each bovine on his feet as it became clear that this fight was to the death.

"Do you think we could separate them with pitch forks?" Uncle R. D. asked my dad.

"No!" my father almost shouted. "At least not now. It would be death to get in there."

The whiteface left the fight and gamboled up the hill as if to head back to his pasture, but then he turned again in an even more deadly lunge at Tommy. No medieval knight in joust ever took a thrust of 1800 pounds of blind fury as did Tommy and then rise to fling his 1500 pounds back at his mortal enemy.

In late afternoon Tommy went down on all fours, and Uncle Oliver's bull did not hesitate to ram him in the flank and the groin. His white face was smeared with clay and gore. Tommy struggled to rise, but he didn't. He bawled a keen, painful bellow.

The whiteface stood back from him and snorted and pawed a final challenge, but Tommy lay silent.

In the end, the whiteface wandered several paces away from Tommy and lay down on the grass. They had spent their strength in the fight. If a heifer had then come into heat, neither one could have been of any service to her.

The next day Uncle Oliver and Uncle R. D. easily drove the whiteface back into his pasture with pitchforks. R. D. and Uncle Oliver rebuilt the fence. Mr. Mark carried water and feed to Tommy for a week before the bull got on his feet again. Then he walked slowly to the shade near the water hole and lay down again. Had Mr. Mark not fed and doctored Tommy he would have died from his wounds.

Remembering that afternoon forty years later, Uncle R. D. said, "They lordy me! Them bulls tore down that fence and liked to kill each other."

The Old Fordson

It stood alone in the barn lot facing the road, its steel wheels worn bright from continual use. Uncle Taylor paid $150.00 cash for it, cranked it, climbed onto the seat, and drove it home.

With angular, steel cleats on its large steel wheels, the old Fordson was a cross between a caterpillar and a tractor, a kind of iron horse that defied absolute obedience. Like its brother, the Model-T Ford, it often did the unexpected.

On a hot day after hours of work, one could turn off the fuel but the kerosene-burning engine would keep right on running. It would stop when it chose to. It could be standing still and mute in the yard with no one near when the old Fordson would chug and move a few inches and then be as still as death itself. Like a malevolent mule, it sometimes kicked the man cranking it hard enough to break his arm. It was even known to backfire and the engine to start firing backwards.

One frosty morning Dad started the tractor and before switching from gasoline to kerosene he put it into reverse. He backed it toward the trailer where I stood waiting. When he and the Fordson drew near, Dad yelled, "Get out of the way! It won't stop!" Before I could clear the big wheel, a steel cleat caught my right shoe and cut through between my toes.

It was on a hot summer afternoon as Uncle Taylor fed

the long, green corn stalks into the silage cutter that I saw the pulley belt between the Fordson and the cutter begin to lurch, and I heard the old Fordson engine miss and stall. The silage cutter had jammed again.

When that happened, Garland Dills, a large, strong tenant farmer, would hold the pulley belt to keep the cutter blades from moving while Uncle Taylor reached his hand into the housing and dug out the green, packed silage, handful after handful.

Suddenly and unexpectedly while Uncle Taylor's hand was in the machine, the old Fordson gave one of its capricious chugs. The pulley jerked, the blades moved, and Uncle Taylor cried, "Garland, back it off my hand!"

Dad leaped over the conveyor belt to Uncle Taylor's side. Mr. Dills pulled the belt in reverse. Blood gushed from Uncle Taylor's hand as he took it from the machine.

Color drained from his face; he staggered and turned toward the house. Dad grabbed him. "Taylor," he said, "lean on the cutter! You need a tourniquet on your arm." And Dad tied his red bandanna handkerchief tightly around Uncle Taylor's upper arm.

Mr. Dills handed another bandanna to Dad and said, "Buddy, tie this below his elbow. It's still bleddin'." Dad took a nail from his pocket and twisted the second knot as he said, "We'll get you to the hospital, Taylor."

With authority in his voice, Dad said to me, "Tell your Aunt Bess that your uncle has cut his hand and that we'll have to take him to the hospital."

With Aunt Bess cradling Uncle Taylor in her arms in the back seat of their '39 Chevrolet, Dad drove out the driveway under the shade of the maples and the giant eucalyptus tree. Mr. Dills and I watched the funnel of red dust rise along the road behind the speeding car. We heard the trumpet horn echo in the valley as the car disappeared around the far bend. Aston Park Hospital in Asheville was over thirteen miles away.

I glanced toward the barn lot. The old Fordson tractor stood silent and serene facing the stilled silage cutter and the half-filled silo.

Uncle Gaston

"Don't be a procrastinator like your Uncle Gaston," my father lectured me in the woodyard. But Don, my best friend, was waiting for me beside his car in our driveway, so I left the stove wood box empty. I could fill it when I came home later.

As I changed from my overalls into dress slacks and splashed Mennen aftershave on the fuzz on my upper lip, I thought of Uncle Gaston. I liked him. He kept the wood split for Aunt Bess's Homecomfort range.

However, I could remember when my Grandmother Morgan had said to my dad, "Go fetch Gaston." Uncle Gaston, her bachelor brother, was living in a horse stall in the old log barn on his farm. That had been a decade ago. It had been a cold and frozen November day. Snow flakes diapered the crotches of the naked tree branches and powdered the frozen ruts in the clay road we followed with the wagon to the Cole farmstead. It seemed like another country from the paved highway Don and I sped down toward Asheville.

There had been bad blood between Uncle Gaston and his brother Jasper over the farm. As Uncle Gaston had inherited the farm, he didn't permit Jasper any part of it, but Uncle Gaston didn't farm it either.

Each winter he read through magazines and seed catalogs and planned all the crops he would plant in the spring. He even ordered seeds and fertilizers and stacked the unopened packages in the large farm kitchen. But come spring Uncle Gaston waited for the perfect day to begin farming. From his magazines he became informed on what to plant, where, how, and why, but he never lifted a spade or turned the soil to start his crops. He procrastinated. The fallow fields grew up in weeds and briars and then saplings. The rail fences rotted down.

As my friend and I drove by the *Asheville Citizen-Times* building I wondered if any editor there knew how my old, great-uncle had waited at his mailbox many mornings for the postman to deliver his newspaper. Uncle Gaston studied the paper from front to back each day and kept up on national and international news.

When Don parked his car near the county courthouse I thought of Uncle Gaston's bold democratic politics. Like the *Citizen-Times*, he was a devoted Democrat, but he didn't vote. At first he didn't pay his poll tax, and finally he failed to register, but that didn't prevent his saying often that "the Republicans would ruin this country."

Of course, Uncle Gaston always opened his mail and kept it neatly organized on the old secretary in the parlor beside the fireplace and the bay window, but while he intended to do something about it, he never did do anything about its contents.

Though he was a fastidious man about his person, he never shaved himself. Each Saturday morning regular as sunrise, he caught the Pisgah and Leicester bus into Asheville where he had a standing appointment at the barber's for a shave and haircut. In Asheville Mr. Gaston Cole was known as a country gentleman of means.

As Don and I stood in line at the ticket booth at the Paramount Theater, a lady carrying by a longhaired Persian cat reminded me that Uncle Gaston loved cats too, and he once kept a multitude of them. One Saturday when he was in town, his brother Jasper went into Uncle Gaston's house with a horse whip, shut all the doors to the kitchen behind him, and proceeded to switch every cat he could corner. As the cats could not escape, each got a merciless beating.

When Uncle Gaston returned home and opened his kitchen door, the frightened and wounded cats fled past him to the safety of the barn, well house, millrace, or granary. A stunned Uncle Gaston stood crying, "Tammy, Honey, Blackie, Sport, Persia, Tucker! Don't you know me?" While Jasper told the story and laughed, Uncle Gaston kept a firm jaw and looked away with his light blue, teary eyes.

I remember stopping with Dad to see Uncle Gaston and his cats and his corner stacked with seed packages before he abandoned the old homeplace and moved into a new frame bungalow. The cedar-shingled roof on the estate house had gone unrepaired for so long that it leaked badly. Uncle Gaston kept buckets standing under the bad leaks. The kitchen porch floor had rotted away and porch roof had sagged. Dad replaced a post under a particularly dangerous roof dip near the kitchen door. The front porch facing the lower meadow and the distant public road had fallen into disrepair and disuse long before.

Uncle Gaston told Dad, "I intended to make some repairs when it quit raining, but then I couldn't tell where it leaked when it wasn't raining."

Uncle Gaston moved into a small, new bungalow set on a ridge with a high porch that stood above the undergrowth in the tall pines around it. Shortly after this move, his nephew Malcolm, a son of Great-uncle Jasper's, was discharged from the army for psychological reasons. Malcolm asked Uncle Gaston if he could farm the land of the Cole estate, but Uncle Gaston quietly and stubbornly refused him any kind of arrangement.

Like his father before him, Malcolm chose a Saturday while Uncle Gaston was away for his revenge. He set fire to the new frame bungalow. Then he shot himself in the leg and walked off into the woods leaving a trail of blood.

Upon his return from town Uncle Gaston found only ashes of his home smoldering in the bungalow's basement. Neighbors who had seen the smoke in the Cole Cove had rushed in, kept the fire from spreading to the forest, and found Malcolm alive but weak from his loss of blood.

It was then that Uncle Gaston gathered a few more pieces of furniture from the estate house and moved into a horse stall in his log barn. In his fastidious fashion, he swept the earth floor clean and hung a mirror over a washstand in the low center shed outside his stall. There were no chinks between the logs of the stall, but the tin roof above the hayloft over the stall was sound. His cats gathered around him, he settled down with his daily newspaper again. Malcolm was committed to an asylum.

On that cold November day in the snow, Dad and I packed Uncle Gaston's bed, chair, and washstand on the wagon, and the mules pulled him and his few possessions to Grandfather Morgan's home. There Uncle Gaston occupied a large upstairs bedroom complete with open fireplace. And there he stayed.

From year to year Uncle Gaston had meant to pay the taxes on his estate, but long neglect of his affairs compounded eventually, and the Cole farm was sold by the county for taxes. Dad had said simply, "The road to hell is paved with good intentions." To me he had often said, "Never put off until tomorrow what can be done today."

Don and I enjoyed the movie. After Roy Rogers rounded up all the cattle rustlers, we stepped out of the theater onto the wet streets glistening in the city's night lights.

When I crawled into my clean, dry bed, the rain on the tin roof drummed me to peaceful sleep.

It was a little after 3:00 A.M. when I felt my bed covers lifted off me and flung to the floor at the foot of my bed.

The switch stung my legs, my back, and my buttocks. Dad had often said that if he had to go to the trouble of cutting a switch, he would do the job right and I would remember it. After he wore the maple switch out on me, he said, "This morning *you* start the stove fire for your mother with wet wood."

I didn't procrastinate.

Aunt Lela

"Deller, I'm praying that Arthur will die soon," Aunt Lela said quietly. I glanced at Mother whose face was expressionless. Aunt Lela continued, "There's no one to care for him if I should die first. You know, he's seventy-six now."

Arthur Mehaffey lived with his sister, Lela, and her husband, Fred Anders, high on the mountain.

Mother cleared her throat, and said, "Leler, I understand. How is Arthur?"

Aunt Lela smiled, "In perfect health as far as I can tell." She sat in a cane-backed rocking chair with a black, leather-bound Bible open on her lap. We were on her porch overlooking the green yard where flowering rhododendron and forsythia bushes grew near the house below the porch. Some apple trees, a plum tree, cherry trees, and a grape arbor bordered the yard. We looked out over the tree tops of the valley beyond. Two beehives stood at the corner of the yard opposite the vegetable garden. It seemed that love and beauty and peace and plenty dwelt there.

"When Fred asked me to marry him," she told us, "I explained that I was taking care of papa and mama and Arthur, and Fred said, 'We'll take care of them together,' and so we have. We raised our two boys. Oder is a preacher now. Did you know that, Deller?" she asked. "Cecil has a good job. They're married now and have children, and they can't work and care for Arthur too. And Fred's had two heart attacks. We're getting old, Deller."

She paused and we sat quietly, each with our own thoughts.

"Arthur couldn't go to one of them nursing homes; they'd not understand him. So I'm asking the Lord to take him before I get unable to care for him."

Mother and I were silent. As a child Arthur had been crippled by acute poliomyelitis which attacked his central nervous system producing paralysis, muscular atrophy in his legs, and physical deformity. Beyond his impaired powers and in spite of his deformities, he had a good mind, a sense of humor, and strong arms.

I recalled Uncle Bud Mehaffey's telling about his brother Arthur when they were young, saying that as children they had all played together, sometimes teasing Arthur. Uncle Bud had laughed and said, "He'd get on all fours and come after us, and if he caught us, we'd not soon get out of his grip."

I had often seen Arthur carried into church in the arms of Fred or Oder and set on the end of a pew near a window where he would sit quietly, grotesque expressions sweeping over his face. He would reach an unsteady hand for a hymnal.

As Mother and Aunt Lela talked I remembered Uncle Bud's story of the illness and death of his first wife. "There I was," he had said, "alone back on that mountain. Our little children were asleep. It was one or two in the morning when Julia grew worse and needed medical care I couldn't hope to get in time. I'd been a circuit preacher, riding my old mule to preach the gospel and working that rough farm. I asked God to help me save her, but she died that night.

"I'd cared for her for days and nights until I was so weary and tired I could hardly stand up. I decided not to disturb the children. I laid her out, put pennies on her eyelids, and crawled into bed beside her and went to sleep. When the children woke up I told them their mother was in heaven and wasn't sick anymore.

"I wondered why God had allowed me, his minister, to lose my beloved wife and the mother of our children. I wondered if he really cared for me." Uncle Bud paused before he added, "I only know that in the many years of my long ministry to many churches no one has ever come to me as desperate as I was when my first wife died. I realize now I was being prepared."

Aunt Lela and Mother had talked about the flowers and the vegetable garden. My thoughts came back to the present when Aunt Lela asked if Mother and I would like to visit with Arthur.

"I can't lift him anymore so he stays in bed," she explained.

Arthur's room was on the back side of the house with two large windows and a view of the yard and mountainside. Arthur's high bed stood against a log-paneled wall. A small stove stood in front of a closed fireplace near the head of his bed. Lilac perfumed the room through the open windows. The room was fresh and clean smelling.

I noticed that Arthur wore a diaper just as a baby might wear. Aunt Lela had placed a newspaper between his diaper and the clean white sheet. "Arthur, this is Deller and her son, Joe, come to see you," Aunt Lela told him. Arthur's face took on several distorted expressions and he extended a twisted hand. Aunt Lela took it gently and held it for Mother to grasp.

"Doolnna," Arthur stammered, then "Yoooah" as I took his hand and held it in mine. In the warm and pleasant room I could see through the thin sheet his large body and his short, useless legs. The light formed a halo around his bald Mehaffey head.

As Mother and I left the porch steps, Aunt Lela pushed a bag of fresh lettuce into my hands.

Back in the car while slowly descending the mountain gravel road and after a long silence between us, I asked Mother what she thought would become of Arthur.

She replied, "More things are wrought by prayer than this world dreams of."

The following March one of Mother's letters included this postscript: "By the way, a few days ago Arthur Mehaffey died quietly in his sleep."

SON

My Brindled Cow

One summer evening months after the great bull fight, my cow, Brenda, came into heat. After I finished at the dairy barn I told Dad, "Brenda is bulling."

"Take her to your Uncle Oliver's bull," he said.

I was thirteen and I had been told countless times to "stay clear of the bulls" when I was in barn lots or pastures. In July Mother and I had picked blackberries in the Jones cove where Uncle Oliver's Herefords then grazed, and we had kept briar patches between us and the bull.

"Will you go with me?" I asked Dad.

"No," he replied with finality, "you're old enough to handle your own stock." But realizing my fear and respect for the bull, he added, "Just keep the cow between you and the bull. He won't be interested in you anyway."

That evening I led my cow on a rope halter by Uncle Oliver's house and he came off the porch to look at my cow. Before he opened the gate he asked, "Isn't your father coming with you?"

"Dad said I'd be all right," I almost whispered.

"Well, be careful," Uncle Oliver warned as he closed the gate behind me and the cow.

Brenda and I followed the creek on past the old log tenant house where Uncle R. D. and Aunt Ruby lived. Brenda kept up a fast pace. Then within sight of Marshall's cabin in the next cove, Brenda saw the bull and bawled to him. I saw him lift his head and look toward us. I stopped at the large moss-covered boulders that lay scattered like abandoned army tanks on the grassy slope.

Brenda bawled and tugged toward the bull, but I held her rope fast. The bull began to trot toward us. I told myself that I could climb onto a giant boulder if the bull gave any hint of charging me.

The big whiteface came steadily on, his great frame jarring the earth. He slid to a stop right beside Brenda. I yanked at her halter rope and kept her between me and the bull.

I had not been that close to him before in the open pasture. His big white head topped with curls and his soft, dreamy, hazel eyes which he half-closed as he rubbed his neck over Brenda's back gave him a tame and gentle look, but I remembered him in his fight with Mr. Mark's Tommy. Also my little brindled cow looked small and fragile beside the great Hereford. I wondered if she could support his weight. After sniffing and licking he mounted her; she merely lowered her head in the mating.

When he dismounted, Brenda stood with a humped back. The bull stood beside her with closed eyes, his skin rippling on his great shoulders. I said, "That's enough, let's go!" and I yanked Brenda's halter rope, but the bovine was as heedless of my instruction as the bull was of my presence.

I pulled at her halter rope. She stood still. I had led her to the bull but it then seemed necessary to drive her away. However, I knew better than to get between her and the bull. So I waited. Soon he mounted her again. Eventually Brenda responded to my tug on her rope and took a few steps toward me. The great Hereford followed. Brenda led easily back through the pasture as long as the bull followed. The three of us ambled along the creek and on toward the gate. The bull seemed all taken with Brenda and stayed close to her. We surely cut an interesting sight; me at the end of the halter rope tugging and watching the bull and the bovines taking their time together, ignoring me.

I began to plan how I would get my cow through the gate and fend off the great bull at the same time, but when it came into view, I saw Uncle Oliver waiting at the gate to help me.

Dad was right. The bull wasn't interested in me.

Blackberry Picking

"If you want some easy blackberry picking, go up yonder in the mountain pasture in the ravine above them boulders where we salt the cattle," Dad advised me. He had overheard my asking Mother if she thought I could sell a few gallons of berries to Mr. Samson at his store. It was a good year for blackberries and I saw it as a chance to make some extra money.

Dot, Dean, and I had picked the briars clean along the orchard fencerow, and Mother had canned all the berries she wanted for cobblers the next winter. Also she had a shelf of blackberry jam in the basement.

"Do you think I could get a dollar a gallon at the store?" I asked Mother.

"Well, you can pick a few gallons and see if people will buy them," she answered. Aunt Ruby had asked me to pick two gallons and she had given me two dollars for them.

"There must be lots of ladies on Newfound," I thought, "who can't get to the good berry patches on these mountains and who would like to can some berries." I decided this was one berry season in which I could get rich.

It was a hot July morning. I gathered two galvanized bale-buckets and a gallon lard pail. The lard pail was a small container I could hold to pick in. I'd empty it into the buckets until I had filled them. It would be all I could carry off the mountain. Also I took a jar of fresh water and a piece of cornbread for an afternoon snack.

I bathed my wrists, ankles, and neck with kerosene oil. Then Mother tied strings around the cuffs of my long-sleeved shirt at the wrists and around my trousers at the ankles above my high-top shoes. The oil would prevent my getting covered with chiggers as I picked in the briars. Also I'd take a bath as soon as I got home to prevent as many chigger bites as possible. I expected to return with five gallons of fresh berries.

Seeing me all prepared, Dad said, "You might as well take some salt for those cattle since you're going on that mountain." He placed a two-pound sack in one of my buckets. "Watch out for any rattlers sunning themselves on those boulders when you put out the salt," he added.

I said, "I will;" and thought to myself, "he's just trying to scare me."

As I climbed the mountain road I often stopped to look back to Uncle Taylor and Aunt Bessie's house and dairy barn. I surveyed the fields that swept upland to the pasture fences.

There below me wrapping the near hillside was the alfalfa field where I remembered stepping on a snake years before. I had been four or five then, walking with Dad and Mother cutting through the lush, blue-green alfalfa field to the strawberry patch. Mom and Dad were carrying armloads of pint baskets for strawberries. In my bare feet, I raced on ahead. Suddenly, I felt a coiling snake roping under my feet.

"Snake!" I screamed as I churned my feet up and down, the surprised snake struggling for freedom. I couldn't seem to jump off him nor could the snake escape my wild dance.

Just as suddenly as I had tangled with the serpent, I was lifted high above him by Mother who had dropped her baskets and raced to my rescue. The snake, free of me, arched down the hill like a glorious black giant inchworm or a living black snake whip undulating away.

As I clung to Mother crying, Dad said, "It's just a blacksnake. He wouldn't bite you."

And Mother soothed, "You're all right. Now be quiet."

I turned my attention back to the blackberries and all the money I could make that afternoon.

When I reached the high, inside curve below the steep, narrow gorge, I climbed under the barbed-wire fence near the culvert. The small cold stream tumbled over the rocks beneath the large boulders where I would put out salt for the cattle.

"Sook, sook, sook," I called to a few Herefords grazing on the steep mountain nearby. They lifted their heads and watched me sprinkle salt on the large rock in their licking places. When they ambled over and began to lick the salt, I sprinkled more salt onto their backs. A steer or two licked at the salt on another's back.

They turned to drink from pools below the small water-falls in the mountain stream. I enjoyed their company, emptied my salt sack, and looked out over the valley far below. The most difficult part of this afternoon was going to be carrying my five gallons of berries back home.

The clumps of blackberry briars grew on both sides of the cold, gurgling stream that tumbled down the ravine. Cow trails laced the mountain pasture like clay ribbons on a giant green skirt. I scrambled up several trails and selected one above a thick clump of tall briars heavy with ripe berries. Dad was right. Each blackberry was as large as one's thumb and they hung in handfuls.

I set the galvanized buckets down on the cow trail, placed the lard bucket bale over my left wrist and picked with both hands. After the first handful tumbled into my tin bucket, I stepped into the briars below the trail from where I could reach a vine bending with berries. The dry leaves crunched beneath my feet but I heard an additional rattle in the leaves not far from my right foot. My shirt sleeves and trouser legs were tangled in briars as I waded in to reach the best berries, but I stood perfectly still and looked to the ground beneath the briars. There, about three feet below me, lay a giant rattlesnake. The scales on his beautiful, silvery skin glistened like a thousand diamonds in the bright sun. He was about three feet long and maybe three inches in diameter. He lay as still as I stood.

I don't remember how I got untangled from the briars and back on the cow trail above, but I remember that the rattler never moved. Perhaps he was used to the cows picking grass above the trail and figured that I'd move on. I did.

The trail wound into the gorge, over the stream, and out on the other side above an even larger patch of briars. There in the shade of a large gum tree and with the ravine and stream between me and the pit viper, I began picking berries again. I could get over these briars more easily by leaning my left arm on the long limb of the gum tree that spread out just above their tops which were at my eye level. I tipped my weight to the limb and reached for a cluster of the largest ripe blackberries I'd ever seen in my life when I saw it move. Inches beyond my hand a long, slick blacksnake stretched along the branch waiting for an unsuspecting bird hungry for berries.

At the same time I saw him, he slid straight down into the briars, one long, slender ebony serpent flowing in a stream, a black living liquid from limb to land. It all happened in slow motion while I watched off balance, my arm resting on the serpent's blind. He disappeared in the briars downhill.

That was enough for me. I didn't like the company in the blackberry patch. I picked up my empty buckets and headed home.

Blackie

I looked down the sights of Dad's 16-gauge shotgun at Blackie, my adopted Labrador. He sat with his head cocked, looking up at me with his large black eyes.

As the scene swam beyond my tears, I recalled a warning: "Don't feed that dog or he'll stay," my father had said. "You can't take in every animal them city folk turn loose on that mountain." It had been a late Sunday evening, and the lovely, lithe Labrador had then sat the same way, with his head cocked looking up expectantly at me from his large black eyes, his tail wagging.

"He's hungry," I told Dad.

"Of course, he's hungry. Let him go beg at some other house. You can't have three dogs." But Blackie became the third stray dog I took in that summer.

Pete, our beagle, had been a perfect farm dog, but he had grown old and had been mauled badly by a pack of younger dogs on his last escapade with a bitch in heat. When he returned home nearly dead, Dad had put him out of his misery.

Pete had walked at the heel, lain on the front porch at night, and never bayed the moon to keep us awake. Told once, "Get the cows, Pete," he walked up the pasture land, found the farthest cow, and walked them all to the barn.

Sometimes old Roan would hide in the woods and stand so still that her cow bell wouldn't ring, but Pete would spot her, sneak up behind her, and bark suddenly at her heels. The startled cow would jump, run out of the trees, her tail high, her bell clanging, her game lost. But Pete never chased her for sport.

It was the stray dogs which city people left on their Sunday afternoon drives that chased the cattle. They ran the cows into fences, over banks, and into ditches. The dogs were cruel to the farm animals, and such dogs had to be trained or shot.

I had a dog graveyard on the ridge above the hog pen. It was in a sassafras grove near the tall timberline and the ghostly silvered trunk of a dead chestnut tree. Each grave was marked with a large rock so that I didn't ever dig in the same spot. Old Pete had not been buried there. His grave was in a corner of the garden.

The first dog I remember burying there was a German shepherd that had come to our house after some city folk let it out of their car on the mountain road. I remember the car came down the road fast by our house, stirring up a tunnel of clay dust, and the shepherd was racing behind, its tongue hanging out eating the dust trying to catch its family's car. Shep had followed the car down the mountain road, but the driver speeded up in the bottomland and Shep gave up the chase at our house.

I had fed him and he had stayed, but he loved to chase cows and cars. He had not been trained to any discipline and though Dad and I whipped him for his sport, he persistently chased cars, cows, cats, and trucks and picked fights with other dogs.

One evening he chased Snowflake into the barbed-wire

fence. After Dad treated her wounds and sewed her torn teat, he got down his 16-gauge shotgun and we walked Shep to the ridge.

Dad said, "He's your dog. Shoot him between the eyes and he won't suffer."

Dad and I dug a deep grave so no other dog would dig him up before he decomposed.

Nevertheless, that experience had not stopped me from collecting dogs or from trying to train them as useful farm animals. The real problem, of course, was that they had been taken as pups for pets and had grown up in a town house without training—"without regard for their breeding," Dad had said. The owners deprived them of discipline and then abandoned them in the country with the notion that the dogs would find a home. Dad often said, "You can't teach an old dog new tricks," but he let me try. I think he always hoped for the best. Anyway, he let me learn about cruelty the hard way.

I called the Labrador Blackie. He was friendly with my other two dogs. Blackie and I played ball together. I pitched, he caught. In his mouth he brought back to me just about anything I threw.

My three dogs that summer were all strays left by Asheville people on their Sunday afternoon drives up Newfound. Brownie was a short-haired chestnut mongrel, even more friendly than Blackie. He liked to shake hands and lick me in the face when I bent down. But I couldn't break him from chasing cars and trucks.

And there was Scotty, a black and white English setter, who loped playfully around the other dogs biting at their ears and barking just to be noticed. When a car pulled into our drive, Scotty leaped and barked to distraction. He too chased about anything that moved, especially cats and chickens. I didn't keep him long enough to train him to catch the chicken Mother selected for me to kill for Sunday dinner.

It was my standing job to get the cows at milking time and my dogs followed me into the pastures. Usually they heeled or loped off in chase of a rabbit, but if a cow began to trot toward the barn, Blackie barked and raced behind her, snapping at her heels. Brownie and Scotty jumped in for sport, and they ran the cows down the hillside, their heavy udders swinging. I screamed, "Blackie, NO! Brownie and Scotty, come here!"

When the cows were cornered or stopped in the barn lot, the dogs came cringing and crawling back to me, their bellies on the grass and their ears back, knowing they were wrong and ready for a scolding.

It was after just such a scene that Dad told me, "Select one of those dogs to train and get rid of the rest. Cows are more valuable than dogs."

After milking that evening, my cousin, Gwen Roberson, stopped by in his pickup. He came into our yard carrying a pure-bred black and white collie pup.

"Uncle Buddy, I heard that you lost your beagle," he said, "and I brought you one of old Tracey's pups. The males were all spoken for, but you can train this collie for a good cow dog."

My dad was not excited about another dog. He said, "Shitfire, Gwen, this boy's got three stray dogs now and not one of them worth the food he eats."

"Uncle Buddy, you need a dog that can be trained to handle cattle," Gwen argued.

"Let's take her, Dad," I pleaded.

Dad studied me a minute and then told Gwen that he appreciated the pup and Gwen's thoughtfulness. To me he said, "We'll take the collie pup, but you must get rid of the strays. I'll give you two weeks to find them a home, but they must be gone in two weeks. We can't train the collie with those older dogs around."

I agreed. I called her Lassie because Dad had read the story, *Lassie, Come Home*, to me and my sisters. Dad said that collies made good cattle dogs because they always meant business. Also he told me that when he was a boy Grandfather Morgan had had a collie bitch which would let down the bars in the fence with her nose on the way to the pasture for the cows.

I began immediately to find homes for Blackie, Brownie, and Scotty. I asked Gwen, "Would you like one of my dogs?"

He only laughed and ran his fingers through his head of blond curls and said, "Good luck," as he climbed into his truck.

Uncle Oliver had sold off some timber, and the next week the large, ten-wheel log trucks rolled slowly by our house on their way to the saw mills, and, of course, Brownie lay in wait to chase the trucks. Brownie's style was to run for the front wheel of a car and snap at it for a few yards, stop still and snap at the rear wheel as it went by. After chasing the large front wheel of his first truck, he stopped to snap at the rear wheel, but the outer and wider rear wheel rolled over his head. His grave lay nearby in my dog graveyard.

Luck was with me when some fox hounds strayed by our house. There were many fox hunters in those days. We often went to sleep at night listening to the "Voice of Bugle Anne" leading the pack of hounds on and off the fox trail. In the aftermath of a fox hunt, some hounds would come by our house. Dad would feed them and put them up in the hen house and wait for the owners to inquire. The men would pay Dad for feeding and keeping their hounds for them. They took Scotty because he was a setter and they thought he could be trained to hunt quail.

Only Blackie was left after two weeks. No one wanted him. I suggested to Dad that we take him back to Asheville and turn him loose, but, of course, Dad said that was to be more cruel to him than his owners were.

I wiped my eyes and beyond the end of the gun barrel, Blackie cocked his head to the other side. I pulled the trigger.

Smoked Out

After I poured the slop into the trough, I sat down above the hog pen where I could see through the cracks and watch the house, the barn, and the woodyard for any sign of my father. He would not see me behind the hog pen.

There were two noisy shoats in the pen slurping the mixture of cornbread, milk, and leftover vegetables Mother had prepared. When they had eaten the slop, I would pour the bucket of fresh water into their trough. Meanwhile, I took out the cotton Bull Durham tobacco pouch and a pack of cigarette wrappers.

Dad had built the hog pen on sled runners so the building could be dragged to new locations from time to time. That way he wouldn't have to haul and scatter hog manure. My dad was clever that way. At that time the pen was in the cow pasture on the ridge above the house next to the timberline, downwind from the house.

I sat on the ground in the shade of a thorn locust keeping an eye on the farm buildings below. Each day I fed the hogs as soon as I had changed my school clothes and always before Dad came in from the fields or barn. Usually he appeared about this time of day. Perhaps he was bringing in the cows. I would stroll back down the hill with my empty buckets when I saw him appear somewhere below.

Dad did not smoke cigarettes or cigars, not even a pipe. He forbade any tenant farmer or hired hand to smoke around the barns. He did dip snuff which he considered safe on the farm. "Don't ever carry matches," he had advised me. "A cigarette butt tossed aside around the dry hay at the barn or chaff of a corn crib can start a fire."

Every farmer in the valley grew an allotment of tobacco and even my cousins, Don and Max, smoked. Uncle Harry, one of my father's older brothers, never objected. He often drawled, "Now, boys, put out those fires before we get to the barn."

Most boys smoked at school; it was the manly thing to do, and besides, I enjoyed putting one over on Dad. He'd never know; he'd never smoke me out. I'd be safe behind the hog pen.

I took a cigarette paper from my small packet. It was so thin I could see through it. I held it curved under my left forefinger, my thumb and middle finger holding the sides. The paper became a trough. With my right hand I poked my finger into the center of the yellow drawstring which gave way and the pouch opened. I sprinkled the fine yellow tobacco into the cigarette paper. Then, holding one end of the string in my teeth, I pulled it tight and tucked the pouch in my shirt pocket. I licked the paper and rolled it into a cigarette. "Not bad," I thought as I admired my handiwork. "A bit lumpy, but I'll get better at this."

From my pocket I took a small box of matches. My cigarette dangled from my lips just like Humphrey Bogart's did in the movies. I struck a match on the side of the box. The breeze on the hillside blew out the flame. I worked at cupping my hands to shield the flame. "Smoking is an art," I thought to myself. I learned to draw as I held the flame to the tobacco. The smoke burned my throat and my nostrils. My eyes watered and I coughed. I took a sip from the bucket of water I had brought for the hogs. Then I leaned back against the tree trunk and puffed away. "What would Dad do if he saw me now?" I wondered.

Above the rustle of tree leaves in the summer breeze and the slurping of the hogs in the pig trough, I heard footsteps behind me, and before I realized it, my father stepped out beside me with an ax over his shoulder. He had been chopping wood back on the ridge.

Stunned, he stopped and looked at me. His mouth dropped open.

I jumped up, threw down my unsmoked cigarette, and ground it under my shoe. Meanwhile, Dad stood staring at me. I couldn't look him in the eye, but I began preparing myself for the inevitable whipping. He had the ax; there were sassafras saplings aplenty under the tall locust, but he didn't lower his ax from his shoulder. He just watched me bracing myself for correction.

Finally, he spoke. "Son, I wished you wouldn't start that habit, but since you're going to smoke, get yourself an ashtray and put it in the house. Don't smoke around the barns; you can burn down everything we have." Then he walked on down the path toward the smoke house to put his ax away.

I poured the bucket of water into the hog trough. A shoat looked up at me and grunted. I was whipped. I did not want to smoke in the house.

I opened the Bull Durham pouch and poured the fine yellow tobacco into the hog trough.

Hillbilly Halloween

It was November 1, 1947, All Saints' Day on the church calendar. I expected to see the results of several Halloween pranks on the way to school, but nothing the likes of which I witnessed that morning.

It had been Dad who had made the first early morning dash to the outhouse only to discover that it had been overturned. The stool sat on its cement foundation, the neat little house placed carefully on its side. Dad called me and we set the outhouse back on its foundation. Brushing his hands together, Dad muttered, "Wonder how many of these were turned over last night."

While my sisters and I waited for the school bus, Mr. Willie Broils drove by much later than usual. Normally he was so punctual that one could set his watch my him. He was returning from the "grave-yard" shift at the Champion Paper and Fiber Company in Canton. Mr. Broils stopped when Dad waved him down. "Why so late, Willie?" Dad inquired.

"Some smartass felled a tall pine across the road in the first turn just this side of the mountain gap," he snapped.

"How dangerous!" Dad said.

"It cut off the traffic between Buncombe and Haywood counties," Mr. Broils complained. "I carry an axe in my car, so I chopped off the top and managed to drive around it. Hope nobody comes barreling down that mountain road or he'll run into the tree or over the bank below that drops straight into that ravine of rocks."

"Oh, law me!" my father exclaimed.

"Well, take care, Buddy," Mr. Broils added and drove on.

As we rode down Newfound on the bus stopping to pick up students, I saw the usual pumpkins smashed on the road, some mailbox posts pulled up or corn shocks piled on them. However, when the bus stopped for the MacElwreath girl, I saw a crew cutting up the trunk and limbs of a giant oak. It had been felled across the pavement that led to Leicester. The main Newfound Valley road had been blocked at both ends by pranksters.

As the bus travelled on toward school, I wondered what we'd find there. I remembered the year we found Mrs. MacIntyre's outhouse standing in front of the main doors. Then there was the year someone locked a horse overnight in Mr. Brown's classroom. It hadn't harmed any furniture, just scattered its droppings over the room.

When we reached school, I first noticed Mr. S. O. Wilde, our principal, and Mr. Gilbert standing on the front terrace and gazing up at the top of the flagpole.

Mr. Gilbert owned the farm that lay beside the school property, and he was the proprietor of the one-man local grocery and gas station. Both his barn and his grocery buildings stood on the Leicester roads.

It was tempting to dash over the bank to his store for candy at recess, but the greater temptation stood under the shed of his large old barn. There he stored a classic, one-horse shay with large black wheels, a cushioned leather-covered seat under a convertible landau top. Its black, shiny horse stays stretched out in front. Every boy loved to climb the barn lot fence and admire his old, unused, dusty buggy. Everybody tried at least once to climb into the seat and look at the world from his grandfather's view.

Boys sometimes teamed up and gave each other rides around the barn lot, three or four boys pulling and pushing as two rode in the buggy. However, Mr. Gilbert objected to anyone's touching or admiring his old buggy. When he saw anyone admiring the buggy, he went into a cursing rage. He had been known to chase boys with a switch or even a horse whip. One could not be sure he wasn't hidden behind the corn crib ready to shout at a trespasser. The risk of getting switched or cursed by old Mr. Gilbert heightened the forbidden joy.

That morning Mr. Gilbert and the principal were gazing up at the buggy resting quietly on top of the flagpole. It was held in its upright position by four guy ropes anchored to posts in the terrace grass. Even Mr. Gilbert was awestruck, silent, and still, while Principal Wilde poked his hands in and out of his pockets and danced around Mr. Gilbert.

As busload after busload of students arrived, the crowd of gazers on the terrace grew larger. Our school building housed first through twelfth grades, and nearly everyone including teachers milled around looking up in disbelief. Mr. Wilde kept saying, "Don't touch the ropes. Stand back."

Someone had earlier called the *Asheville Citizen-Times* and a reporter and photographer arrived to take pictures and interview Mr. Wilde and Mr. Gilbert. "How did they do it?" was asked over and over again as new people joined the crowd. How to get the shay down safely became the problem no one seemed able to solve.

The bell rang and we were herded into our classrooms, but even there we gathered at the windows to look up at the buggy swaying in the breeze. Our school was a two-story building, but the large, metal flagpole soared higher yet.

Mr. Wilde's voice came on the P.A. system. It was very calm, but he could not hide his delight in the perfect, waggish trick someone had played on Mr. Gilbert. He said, "Now, we've all enjoyed the prank with Mr. Gilbert's buggy, but it is time now to raise the flag. Of course, we can't do that until the buggy is taken down. I've talked with Mr. Gilbert and we agree that we've all seen a clever piece of engineering.

"There will be no reprisals for the boys who did this if they'll come forth now, take Mr. Gilbert's buggy down from the flagpole, and return it to his barn."

Immediately the Cox brothers from the great dairy farm in Green Valley got to their feet and sauntered down to the terrace. The oldest boy stepped to the base of the flagpole, took the end of a rope in his teeth, and shinnied up the pole, the buggy and him swaying gently at the top. He threaded the rope through the pulley wheel and then tied it to the buggy frame.

Down he slid and took the other end of his rope on the ground. One by one the other Cox boys released the guy lines and together they brought the buggy down the pole slowly, like lowering the flag.

When the wheels touched the pavement, from every window the large audience applauded its heroes and saints.

Kate, the Shrew

A mule can cause one to lose his patience, his dignity, and his religion.

My Uncle Taylor had such a mule he called Kate. She was a fiery, nervous, leathery animal who leaped in the traces against a load. Dad had another, a large monkey-mouthed male he called Tom. Under Dad's firm hand they became a good team. Tom was calm, strong, and slow, and he taught Kate to lean forward and let her weight move the wagon.

Eventually Kate learned to work with Tom and to lend her muscle and weight to his pace. They seemed to love each other. When in the lot, they often stood end-to-end like horses do on vacation. Kate was unpredictable, but Tom never seemed surprised if she suddenly gave him her heels in the rib cage.

Those mules were the horsepower on our farm. On winter days we hitched them to the sled and went for firewood. In early spring they pulled the bull-tongue plow turning the soil. They dragged the disk as well as the drag harrow back and forth across the fields. They drilled wheat and rye and planted and cultivated corn. In summer, as a team, they pulled the mowing machine and the hay wagon.

Often Dad and I worked together in the garden and the cornfield, each with a mule and a row cultivator. They and we labored steadily back and forth across the acres.

By late afternoon the mules would hint that it was time for the barn. When headed in the direction of the barn they walked with a lively step but when turned for another round, their pace was slow and stubborn.

Late one afternoon Dad and I were plowing corn, the last cultivating before the plants grew tall and the leaves met in the aisles between the rows. We drove the mules by the barn. Dad took Tom on to a small garden patch to work, and I took Kate to the last small strip of corn along the dry branch that paralleled the mountain road. The mules could not see each other, but Kate could see the barn and came alive each time I turned at the upper end of the field. I took the reins from around my neck and shoulders and drew them tight, holding one in each hand while gripping the cultivator handles, but Kate took the bit into her teeth and strode on. It was all I could do to keep the plow beside the corn. I, too, wanted to finish, but Kate let me know that she was put upon—alone with me when Tom was surely basking in the sun. She was not going to endure it. But a fourteen-year-old boy can be as stubborn and headstrong as a mule; Kate and I had time to finish before milking and I wanted to do it right.

I sank the plows of the cultivator deep into the soil. She showed her muscle and pulled. The wood in the singletree and plow tongue bent. She wasn't tired or done-in, but she had her rights. I jerked the reins and sawed the bit. At the end of the field she leaped toward the bank turning for the barn. I reined her in, cutting her mouth with the bit as I bent her head back to the row. I caught her wide, wild-eyed look as she peered around her blinder. We were at war.

My armor was only a light cultivator and old leather reins patched together with leather string, adequate for the faithful, benevolent horse, adequate for Kate when we had polite conversations of *gee* and *haw* and *click-click* or *whoa*.

Normally, Kate and I could turn row after row and not break one stalk of corn, but in this turn, we devastated a circle of plants. She stomped on every plant she could reach. No mare was ever more prissy as she tossed her mane and arched her tail. Her well-kept coat glistened in the hot afternoon sun, those hips strong and stormy.

Having lost this little battle and learning that we weren't leaving the field, Kate turned into the next row. I had to slap her with the reins to start her up again. She seemed exhausted. She had lost her strength to pull. I had no trouble guiding the plow. Every stalk was wrapped in loose soil. Poor Kate stopped several times to rest as we strove wearily up the hill.

We managed a perfect turn at the top. Then Kate came to life again. *If that stupid boy couldn't understand that it was "quittin' time" for her, she'd just go on to the barn with him and the plow the nearest way.*

A mule who runs is never any good again, and I wasn't going to permit it. I had to win this battle too. I jerked her into the row. She leaped forward. I kept one hand on the plow, guiding it to the center of the row to save some corn. I sawed at the reins. Kate was undaunted. She had the cultivator out of the soil and me out of patience. We cut a destructive course toward the barn. I can't remember any of the impolite things I said to her but I remember angry tears smeared my face. I abandoned any notion of saving the corn or the cultivator. I sawed the bit in her mouth until she reared up on her hind legs and backed into the plow. I whipped her with the loose ends of the reins as hard as I could. She was at my mercy and I was fresh out. *No dumb ass was going to make a monkey out of me.*

Over the fray, I heard the familiar bray of Tom. Dad had arrived to help finish the plowing. At once Kate and I stood still. She was immediately submissive, the obvious victim of a teenager's cruelty and fury. She stood with drooped head in a tired, weary, patient stance and gave Tom a low nicker. When I loosened the reins, she gave me one of her forgiving and accepting looks.

Not so my father. "Can't you work an animal without getting her all upset?" he snarled. "Take Tom and I'll take Kate." He added, "I don't think your Uncle Taylor would take kindly to your treatment of his mule."

* * *

It was some years later when on leave from the Marine Corps I stopped by to see Uncle Taylor and Aunt Bess. Tractors had taken over with their horsepower, but I saw Kate strolling and nipping at grass in the barn lot.

"What do you use Kate for these days?" I asked Uncle Taylor.

"Nothing," he replied. "She's worked long enough."

We rose from the yard chairs and walked toward the white plank fence. We watched Kate switch her tail and stomp at a few flies. She gave us a long look and then ambled over to the old Fordson tractor standing idle in the barn lot where she paused. Confronting the machine, she glanced back at us, tossed her head and shook it in a kind of horse laugh before she walked on toward the barn.

A slow smile swept Uncle Taylor's face and he said flatly, "She's retired now."

A Tale

Normally, I milked a cow and kept my mouth shut, but that morning Aunt Bess was milking the cow in the stanchion behind me and I wanted to tell her my story before I left the dairy barn to catch the school bus.

It was an early January morning. The cows had slept in the lounging barn the night before and some had soiled their udders in wet manure as they lay in the closed shed.

I had used three buckets of soapy water to wash the udders in the row of cows standing in the stanchions. I had not bothered to wash the manure from the cows' tails; there were no flies to swish in the winter cold.

The old battery radio, its knobs replaced with pennies in the slits, stood on the high shelf; Reed Wilson on WWNC played his theme song, "Nothing Could Be Finer than to be in Carolina in the Morning."

I had sat down on a three-legged metal stool, set my milk bucket on the cement under my cow's udder, placed her tail between my knee and her leg, and leaned my head against her flank. With my head and knee I could sense any intended stomp or kick and prevent her hoof from catching my milk pail. As she let down her milk I gripped one teat in each hand and made the galvanized bucket ring with streams of warm milk.

The cow leaned and strained against the stanchion as she licked the grain and cottonseed meal in her manger. I watched the milk foam and rise in my pail.

As Aunt Bess sat milking, I turned my face aside and said, "Aunt Bess, did Uncle Taylor tell you what happened yesterday when we went into Southern Dairies for our milk checks?"

She knew, of course, but she asked, "What happened?"

"When we went into the office and up to the front desk where you get your milk check, Miss Peterson saw us and said, 'Mr. Sluder, here is your check,' but she didn't seem to have a check for me.

"Uncle Taylor then said, 'This is Joe, my partner that I told you about.'"

Partner had been a rather elaborate word for me, the boy who helped at the dairy and did the washing up. A few months before, Uncle Taylor had asked Southern Dairies to give me my own can number which meant I could put the milk from my cows into my own can and receive a check in my name. I preferred that arrangement to getting an allowance for my help at the barn.

Soon after I had my number 40, the State Department of Agriculture established a milk base, or a limit on the number of dairy businesses, by declaring that only those farmers with a creamery number could sell grade-A milk. This action controlled the supply of milk and thereby kept the price up for the farmer. It meant that I had a valuable and coveted business.

As I continued my story, I said, "Miss Peterson asked us if we could wait because someone wanted to meet me."

Dad finished milking a cow, and as he passed me with his heavy bucket of milk he said, "You didn't wash the manure out of that cow's tail behind you. Less talk and more work if you're going to milk your eight cows before that school bus comes."

I went on with my story. "When Miss Peterson returned, she brought a very nice man who, she said, was the president of Southern Dairies!"

"You mean Mr. Chandlers," Aunt Bess said.

"Yes," I went on, "and he said that he wanted to meet me and present my check to me because I was the youngest dairyman in all of Southern Dairies!"

I opened my mouth to say, "They took my picture with the president for the newspaper," when Jersey Bell's tail, caked with wet, green cow manure, swung directly into my open mouth. Even my cheeks and ears were wrapped in it.

I gagged and grabbed the milk bucket from under my cow, set it against the wall, and reached for the water hose.

Aunt Bess laughed and laughed, and Dad quipped, "Even a fish wouldn't get into trouble if it'd keep its mouth shut."

NEIGHBOR

Anner, Ellie, and Mark Daves

I stopped rattling the empty milk pails and stood perfectly still on the path through the tall grass damp with morning dew. The mountains echoed the music of Mr. Mark Daves's yodeling, "Eee o de ladee, O de ladee, O de ladee hee." The echo came back off the Hutchinson mountain, then the Jones cove faintly repeated the falsetto for me. I listened in the misty morning air as Mr. Mark varied his yodel and played with the echoes.

The sun had touched the mountaintops above the wisps of morning fog that curled in the deep coves and rose along the creek bank in the bottomland.

"EEE O DE LADI," Mr. Mark sang, and the echo returned "eee o de ladi." "EEE O DE LAA (ee o de laa) DE HEE (de hee)." Maybe someone was standing on the Jones mountain imitating his every sound as one of my sisters sometimes followed me around and repeated everything I said.

It was not the first time I had stopped to listen to Mr. Mark's songs as I worked. Sometimes at evening he broke into a Scotch or Irish ballad as he strolled home from his horse barn, but yodeling was his early morning song and our valley was its perfect echo chamber.

I stood on the path to our milk barn. Across the bottomland any spoken word carried clearly. We could even hear Anner's "Dad blast it, be still," to a milk cow or Ellie's soft "*Cush, cush,*" to a reluctant heifer.

"Mornin', Mark." I heard Dad's usual call from the hillside on which our barn stood.

"Think it'll rain, Buddy?" he asked back. "This hay could use another day to cure." His alfalfa and orchard grass below the house and barns lay heavy over the field after yesterday morning's mowing. The hay spread to the creek banks, its sweet fragrance drifting on the morning dew.

"Maybe not." My father was surveying the Southern sky.

"Well, Lord willin' and the creek don't rise, I'll get it up by tomorrow." Mr. Mark whistled his way on toward his barn.

The Daves clapboard home stood on a rise above the fields, the large horse and cow barn rose against the Daves mountain pasture which butted up against the higher Jones and Bearwater mountains. The craggy, rocky cliffs high against the blue sky glistened in the bright morning sun.

The bails of my milk buckets began their squeaky rattle again as my bare feet sought safe steps on the plank foot bridge.

"Hey, Della! Cows are ready," Dad called to Mother who was already on the path behind me. Even though Mother had hay fever, she always appeared at the barn and milked her cows while her eyes teared, her nose ran, and she sneezed violently. As soon as we finished, she and I took the milk to the kitchen, strained it, and placed the glass containers in the milk race.

As Dad turned the cows out to pasture, I heard Miss Anner, Mark's older sister, calling her chickens, "BID-DEE, Biddy, Biddy, Biddy, Biddy, come on, Biddy," her voice as clear as if she had been in our yard.

I had been over there at feeding time often enough to know that she was flinging dampened corn meal on the hard earth in front of the chicken house, and the Rhode Island red hens were racing to her. In my mind's eye, I could see a hen scratching in the corn row, jerk its head up at her call, turn and stretch its long neck out front, and race toward Anner, its wings flapping. To see Anner walking from barn to house was to see a woman wading in a surf of red and white hens, the rooster prancing proudly on the fringe of the flock.

Then I heard the shoats squeal and clamor and rush the trough as Ellie approached the pen with two heavy buckets of slop mixed with corn meal. Those hogs would be among the largest at hog-killing time next November. Ellie was the younger of the two sisters with whom Mark lived. She tended to listen quietly at conversations and to work hard. I never ever heard her sing.

After we ate the noon meal which we called dinner, Mother and I set the washed bushels of fresh picked corn-field beans in the shade of the locust trees and began string-ing and breaking them for canning later.

Mr. Mark brought out his team of beautiful horses, hitched them to the rake and rode across his hayfield turn-ing the alfalfa into windrows. He would use the hand fork later and shock the hay for easy loading on the wagon.

We saw Anner and Ellie leave their yard with Jip, the dog, and stroll down their drive toward the creek and disappear behind the tall corn in the field between us and Mark's hayfield. We were quietly snapping beans and tossing them into the tin bowl when Lassie, our collie, gave a welcome *"yap"* to Jip strolling ahead of Anner and Ellie coming up the gravel road toward us.

Both women wore long print dresses with clean bib aprons that showed the wear of many washings and, of course, the fading from hanging on the clothesline in the hot summer sun. Each also wore homemade brim bonnets that shaded the entire face from the sun with a bow string tie under the chin. Anner was then seventy-six and Ellie twelve years younger. They stopped from time to time and looked over the wire fence between the road edge and their corn, pointing at plants and talking quietly together. Ellie picked some honeysuckle in bloom and carried it along, sniffing its fragrance as they drew closer to us and our yard bean factory.

Lassie and Jip smelled each other over carefully and decided they would lie down and listen to the talk.

"We came over to sit a spell, Deller," Anner said.

Mother laid her newspaper full of beans off her lap onto the grass, stood and said, "How nice to see you. Joe, bring two chairs from the table."

They sat next to the containers of green beans. "Ellie, we can help Deller while we rest," Anner began, and picked up a large handful of beans and dropped them on her apron in her lap. Her nimble fingers began to strip and break the pods. Mother's protests that it could all wait were kindly ignored.

"Them twins and that baby make a lot of work, ain't it, Deller," drawled Ellie. "Hit takes a heep o' cookin' to feed a man and them chillin', ain't it?"

"Where's them twins, Deller?" Anner inquired.

"They're at Bessie's playing with Ruth Anne."

"And that baby? What did you call her?" My new sister had been born in February.

"Glennan," said Mother. "Glen for my brother and Nan for my mother. They both wanted me to name her after them."

I put in that Dad had nicknamed her already and Mother explained, "Buddy was taking that new patent medicine when I got pregnant and so he calls her Hadacol."

Anner laughed at the joke.

Ellie held one hand over her mouth as she laughed. "Well, that's Buddy, ain't it?"

"Ellie don't feel no good this atternoon," Anner explained as Ellie got up and walked to the edge of the yard beside the road. She stood there with her back to us, held her long dress and apron back as she vomited up her lunch. When the spasms passed, she wiped her mouth and chin with her soft apron and walked back to her chair. "Somethin ' I et, ain't it?" she suggested. I handed Ellie the glass of water Mother had sent me to get.

Clouds out of the west darkened the distant mountains then floated across the valley. We watched their shadows sweep over the wheat field, the cornfields, the gardens, and the hayfield where Mr. Mark was finishing his raking. He unhitched his team and left the rake at the edge of the field below the barn. The horses turned loose in the lot, he returned alone to the field with his pitchfork to shock the hay.

"I'm a-feared it'll rain and get Mark's hay wet, ain't it?"

Ellie said as she glanced across the mountaintops. "Looks like rain back on the Pinnacle, ain't it?" she observed.

"We better be a-goin', Deller. Me and Ellie can help shock hay. Feelin' better, Ellie?" Anner asked.

"Much better, Sister, and thanks for the drink, Deller. Water rinses the stomach, ain't it?"

Carrying a peach pie that my mother gave them, Anner called to Jip and they walked under the shade trees down our yard and onto the gravel.

Before Mother and I got the beans ready for canning, hay shocks stood in neat lines across Mark's hayfield where windrows earlier lay. I heard Mark whistle for the horses, and I saw him and Ellie return to the field with the team and wagon, Jip tagging along behind. Then while Anner slopped the hogs, milked the cows, and called the chickens, Ellie forked hay to Mark who packed it on the wagon.

When Dad got our cows into the barn for the evening milking, the gray clouds were gathering close on the Bear-water and Jones mountains. A cool breeze stirred the corn tassels and the wheat swayed gently. Studying the clouds and watching our neighbors in the field, Dad said, "Joe, get my good hay fork and go help Mark and Ellie get as much hay up as you can before that rain hits. Your mother can milk your cows for you."

The hay was cured perfectly, light and sweet to smell. I put my fork in on the other side of the shock and with Ellie lifted layer after layer up to Mr. Mark on the wagon.

We three forked the load into the barn loft and returned the team to the field. The cooler wind announced a summer storm. Corn across the creek swayed in the fresh breeze.

Dark, heavy clouds rolled on the mountaintops and the air smelled damp. Distant thunder rumbled somewhere behind the Bearwater.

Anner, chores finished, appeared with her fork raking up the loose wisps of hay and laying them on the wagon. Not touching the reins, Mr. Mark talked the horses from shock to shock of fragrant hay. Suddenly, my father, with a manure fork in his hand, appeared on Ellie's side of a shock of hay and said, "Ellie, let me handle this one."

"Can you get it all on that load, Mark?" asked Dad as we strained together lifting half a shock up to Mr. Mark at each toss.

"I can pack it if you can toss it, Buddy," Mark drawled. "Throw that next one on the back end."

The load grew heavy as the hay piled higher; we pitched each bunch to Mark's feet where he tromped it down. My father knew right where to toss each forkful so that Mark wouldn't have to replace it.

Anner said, "You don't need me. I'll get the supper on." She called Jip and made her way across the stubble field toward the house, pitch fork held like a shepherd's staff.

Lightning cracked the dark sky. Thunder clapped and echoed. A few big drops of rain hit us as the last shock went up on the load. Mr. Mark took the reins, waved them and ordered "get up" to his team.

The horses seemed to lift the heavy wagon as they turned up the slope toward the barn, their strong hips straining together while the hay wagon rocked back and forth with Mr. Mark standing high above, giving the team the reins.

"Many thanks, Buddy, 'til you're better paid," he called back as he headed the team and wagon for the shed between his hayloft and the stock stalls.

Her long dress billowing in the rising wind and holding the brim of her bonnet with both hands, Ellie said, "Tell Deller that peach pie's a-gonna taste mighty good atter supper, ain't it?" She trudged behind the wagon to help Mark unharness the team.

Dad and I cut across the creek and through the corn at a trot toward home.

The rain came sweeping down the mountainsides in sheets, over the upland pasture, across the high fields, and then pelted the bottomland. On the tin roof of our kitchen the rain drummed a soft staccato over our supper. The creek would rise by the time we finished our peach pie.

Bud Bonnom

As I walked up the long tree-lined drive to Aunt Carrie and Uncle Oliver's home, I passed Bud Bonnom, alone, patiently swinging his scythe as he mowed the honeysuckle and weeds along the fencerow.

I shouted, "Hello, Bud!" but he didn't hear me as he concentrated on his work and his own thoughts. I knew, too, that he was nearly deaf.

Bud was a gnome-shaped, hunchbacked, simple-minded man in his late sixties. He lived with Uncle Oliver and Aunt Carrie who had taken him in, years before I was born. Dad told me it was after Bud's sisters had cheated him out of his part of the farm he and they had inherited.

I knew, too, that Bud did everything that Uncle Oliver and Aunt Carrie asked him to do. He split the wood for the cook stove and the open fireplaces of their big house. (Once he cut off a little bit of both ends of a stick of firewood so it would fit into the fireplace.) He shucked hundreds of bushels of field corn during the winter months under the great sheds of Uncle Oliver's barns. He kept the thistle chopped out of the mountain pastures, and he kept miles of fencerows and creek banks mowed. Almost single-handedly, he kept Uncle Oliver's great farm a show place.

After supper on summer evenings, he mowed the lawn with an old reel-type push mower. Regardless of the size of the task, Bud worked patiently and steadily and quietly until he finished it. I never heard him sing to himself as he worked, but I did hear him talk to himself or to the faithful dog that stayed near his side.

"Get him, Brownie!" Bud would scream if a rabbit jumped up from the weeds. He would watch the chase, laugh, and return to swinging his scythe.

Aunt Carrie sat on a glider on her large front porch, and I swung in the swing as we visited and looked out over the fields of corn and wheat and alfalfa and tobacco wilting under the hot summer sun. We also watched Bud swing his scythe at the stubborn weeds along the rocky fencerow just beyond the grape vineyard at the edge of the yard. His long-sleeved shirt and faded overalls were wet with perspiration, but the tall weeds kept falling rhythmically to the swish of his scythe.

Suddenly, Aunt Carrie said, "Joe Dicky, take some cold water and a piece of ginger cake out there to Bud."

When she brought it from the kitchen, she said, "Tell Bud to sit in the shade and rest a spell. It's too hot to work; it must be ninety-five degrees."

Bud stopped swinging his scythe when Brownie barked at me. His humpback prevented him from standing straight or from raising his head upright. He looked at me from a red, sweat-smeared face, his mouth hanging open.

I shouted at him, "BUD! AUNT CARRIE SENT YOU SOME WATER!"

I handed him the cool jug. He lay down his scythe, took the jug in both hands, pulled out the cork, and then drank from the jug. The cool water poured into his mouth and over his chin and streamed to the ground. After he drank plenty, he put the cork back into the jug's throat and set it in the shade of a post.

"Here's some gingerbread too!" I shouted.

"I don't want no gingerbread. YOU EAT IT." His voice was high and loud.

"Aunt Carrie said to tell you that it's too hot to mow today. You ought to rest in the shade," I told him.

"Huh?" He peered at me, his mouth open.

I shouted louder, "AUNT CARRIE SAID TO REST! IT'S TOO HOT TO WORK!"

"Oliver told me 'mow this fencerow,'" he shouted back at me. "I can't mow settin' in the shade. Oliver said 'mow this fencerow!'"

He picked up his scythe, placed the handle end on the ground, pulled his whetstone from his pocket, and rubbed the stone along the sharp blade. I stood and listened to the grinding of the stone and then watched Bud resume his labor.

As I strolled back to Aunt Carrie, smelling the fresh cut honeysuckle, I thought about another side to Bud which I saw every Sunday. Neither Aunt Carrie nor Uncle Oliver attended church, but every Sunday morning Uncle Oliver shaved Bud and trimmed his iron-gray hair. After he bathed, Bud put on a clean shirt and overalls and walked to our house where he knocked at the kitchen door.

"I've got chewing gum for the girls," he always announced to my dad who sat in his rocker by the fireplace. "The girls all like me! Hee! Hee!" he would say to Dad with a laugh.

"You're just a ladies' man, Bud," Dad would tease him.

"Some men have all the luck."

"Hee! Hee! Hee!" Bud would laugh and ask my mother, "Deller, would you like some chewing gum?"

Of course, Mother took a stick, read the label, and shouted to him, "Juicy fruit! You'll be a hit with all the women today, Bud." And Bud would laugh his high "Hee! Hee!," his face aglow with gratitude.

With Bud beside her, Mother drove our convertible A-Model Ford to Zion Hill Baptist Church. The twins and I rode in the rumbleseat.

In church, Bud sat quietly and apart on his bench during the services, his face wrinkled and twisted in painful concentration on the speaker's words. He stood and he sat as the congregation did during the worship, but he never sang a note, never prayed a prayer, never read a line, never said an audible "amen."

It was after the services when everyone was greeting everyone that Bud's face became angelic.

"Bud, did you bring me some chewing gum? What kind of gum do you have today?" the women asked him. Bud laughed his "Hee! Hee!," opened pack after pack, and handed a stick to each woman who smiled at him.

"Thank you, Bud."

"Thank you, Bud."

"Thank you, Bud."

Mr. Roy Sharp would say, "Bud, you're spoiling these women with that chewing gum."

Bud would laugh his "Hee! Hee!" and say, "Yeah." And Mr. Sharp would pat him gently on his humpback.

We were often the last to leave the churchyard because

Mother would wait and watch Bud give all his gum away.

When I reached Aunt Carrie's porch and sat down in my seat on the swing again, we both sat silent a bit and watched Bud swing his scythe in the simmering sun.

Almost to herself, Aunt Carrie said, "Dear, old, faithful Bud Bonnom. If the Lord don't call him home first, he'll labor on 'til Gabriel toots."

Marshall Gregg

"There ain't never no cuss words on Marshall Gregg's lips," Aunt Carrie told me. "No swear words. The worst he'll say is 'By Ned.' I've seed him miss a nail and hit his thumb with a hammer and all he'd say is, 'By Ned, that hurts.' Told me once he heard the Good Book says, 'Thou shalt not take the name of the Lord thy God in vain,' and so he don't never do it. He's allus down at the barn afore daylight feeding the mules so's they'll be ready to harness when Oliver's eaten his breakfast. He works long and hard, one of the best tenant farmers your uncle's ever had."

"Then why's he missing now that the hay's ready to haul?" I asked.

"That's none of your business, Son," Aunt Carrie assured me, her voice softer. "It's Marshall's business and someday when you're older, you'll understand." There was a conspiracy of silence regarding Marshall's periodic disappearances from the farm. Back in the field I pried out a line from Dad on the subject of Marshall's absence.

"He'll be back in a week or two. We'll get on without him."

It was clear that Dad considered me old enough to do a man's work in the field and too young to understand some mystery about Marshall's life. But I missed his lively step, his taking the heavy part of a pitching job and his talk.

As long as I had known him, Marshall had lived alone

on Uncle Oliver's farm—first in a log smoke house over the root cellar and then in a log cabin that Uncle Oliver built for him. It stood on a ridge back toward the Jones cove with a vista of the farms in the valley below and the hills of Dad's pastures, orchard, and woodland on the horizon.

Marshall was a lithe, thin, and trim red-headed Irishman "with a gift for gab," Aunt Bess would say. He always wore a red and white bandanna around his neck. In the fields his vest and ornate leather boots brightened our time and he had over seventy years of stories and songs and wit to make the day's work with him a holiday. Where would a seventy-year-old man go for a few days? And why?

"He isn't sick, is he, and in the hospital?" I inquired.

Dad, on the wagon, stood at rest a moment and leaned on his fork stuck in the hay. "No, he's not sick . . . or maybe he is sick. Leastwise, leave it alone and pay attention to that fork in your hands. You're lifting too much at once, and you're going to stick that fork in my leg the way you're pitching blind."

With Marshall gone, I was teamed with Uncle Gaston to load the hay. He never seemed interested in finishing a job. He would often stop lifting hay, lean on his fork handle, and begin some story he had read in the Asheville Citizen-Times—how the Republicans would ruin this country. My father often said, "Uncle Gaston knows more about what's going on in Washington than he knows about what's growing on the farm."

Uncle Gaston lived with Aunt Bess and Uncle Taylor and took care of their wood splitting. Everyone was respectful to him as he was in his early eighties. I wasn't interested in hearing how great Franklin Delano Roosevelt had been as President nor the latest buck that stopped on Harry Truman's desk, subjects Uncle Gaston discussed constantly. Also, he kept talking even when his upper plate of false teeth dropped out of the roof of his mouth periodically. He would push it back up with his tongue and go on with his criticism. He had all his teeth removed some years before and had a full set of false teeth made immediately, before his gums had reshaped, and so his teeth would not stay in place for more than a few minutes. It made listening to the wonders of Democratic politics somewhat tedious, especially in the hayfield.

Marshall would have said, "By Ned, Gaston, why didn't you run for the Senate? You'd be our most valuable man in Washington. You could have made the WPA build me one of those fancy outhouses at my cabin." And Marshall would have kept right on working.

Uncle Gaston was slow and he let me do most of the lifting. Then, too, he would rake up every little straw before we moved on to the next shock. I was getting out of sorts—no solution to the mystery of Marshall's absence and no foreseeable finish to haying with Uncle Gaston. I quit trying to talk and pitched hay as fast as I could.

As Uncle Gaston poked along picking up every wisp of hay behind the wagon, I began to lift the shocks up to Dad before Uncle Gaston caught up to help. Dad cautioned me to slow down, that he couldn't pack it so fast. In my sullenness, I ignored him.

Also, in order to lift large, heavy bunches alone, it was necessary to put my back to the wagon and lift them up over my head and toss them behind me. Dad had to watch out for the sharp prongs of my hay fork.

"Slow down," he ordered.

I lifted another layer up without regard for where he was standing. In the handle of the fork I felt a sharp prong dig into Dad's leg. I pulled the fork back quickly.

"Shitfire! I told you to slow down and watch what you're doing," he blazed at me as he slid down the hay off the wagon. He kept a keen hickory switch for the mules at the head of the wagon, and he had not forgotten to bring it with him to the ground.

He didn't give me any more information about Marshall. He gave me a thrashing. I was too old to cry so I stood mute under the blows on my back and legs.

Uncle Gaston caught up with the wagon about the time Dad's anger and energy were subsiding. "Buddy, what?" I heard him blurt out before his teeth popped right out of his mouth. "Enough, Buddy, stop," he pleaded. Without any teeth and his lips flapping, he laid a trembling hand on Dad's shoulder. "What's the boy done?"

Dad pulled up his overall leg, spit tobacco juice into his hand, and rubbed it onto the wound. He gave me a fierce look and climbed back onto the wagon.

Uncle Gaston found his false teeth in the hay stubble, dusted them off, and laid both plates back into his mouth.

We finished loading the wagon in silence.

* * *

Sometime after wheat harvest, I noticed a single blue line of smoke rising from the mountain forest halfway up the slope toward Hooker's Gap. William Robertson, one of the most uncivil men on Newfound, lived over there in the cove back up next to the forest line. Of course, he was distilling grain into whiskey again. I had seen those lines of smoke in the hills and the "white lightning" in fruit jars more often than I had seen the make-shift stills, but I would recognize one if I happened upon it while hiking in the hills. Eventually the county sheriff located his illegal corn liquor distillery and confiscated it.

That evening at supper, I said, "When I came across the top of the hill from Uncle Taylor's dairy barn, I didn't see any smoke coming from Marshall's cabin."

"Yes, Marshall's gone again," Dad said flatly.

When supper was over, I said, "There's a Gregg boy at school who told me that Marshall is his grandpaw."

"Yeah, Marshall had a lot of grandchildren," Dad said. "Even great-grandchildren, I reckon, by now."

Marshall was decades older than my father, but I asked, "Did you know Marshall when he was married?"

"Well, yeah." Dad studied me a moment. "He never got any divorce so I guess he's still married. Uncle Mort Jones told me once that Marshall had loved only one woman. She had red hair too, and was a good looker in her day. She'd turn the head of a man and she knew it. Men liked her, but Marshall married her, and they had five children all quick-like."

I sat very still, almost holding my breath so Dad would tell me more.

"They had a stormy marriage. Some said they'd fight like cats and dogs and Katy would leave him with the kids, then she'd come back home and they'd make up and be happy awhile together. Marshall would work harder than ever, but it wouldn't last because Katy had another man, who loved her too, and she couldn't make up her mind between 'em."

"Did you know that man?" I guided him on.

"Bud Brooks, who is about the same age as Marshall and Katy, was a handsome young man then, with black hair and black eyes and he wanted Katy too. Katy left Marshall to go to live with Bud. Marshall nursed and clothed his kids and went on working on farms for other people.

"Once when Katy came back to him and the children, someone told Marshall that he was living in sin because his wife had been with another man, that he'd have to marry her again. He couldn't read nor write, but he always tried to do what was right. So he married Katy in the church again—married the same woman twice without ever getting a divorce." Dad sat still and quiet looking at the poker on the hearth. Then he said, as if to himself, "He's not had an easy life, but he don't ever complain."

"Then he goes to visit his children and grandchildren when he's away?" I asked.

"Sometimes, yes, I guess he does," Dad said, but I knew by his tone that I was "wide of the mark," as Marshall would say.

* * *

In the fields cutting and spudding tobacco, Marshall would sing and whistle as he worked and kid me if I were with him. "Little Buddy, let's you and me show these other fellers how to work," and we had fun turning the work into a game. My dad and Uncle Taylor let us finish our row first—the old man and the boy, the best team in the field.

When we hung the heavy tobacco high in the tobacco barns, Marshall would climb into the rafters, walk the loose planks, and place the tobacco sticks just right for the months of curing to come. He was as nimble and sure-footed as many men decades younger than he. In the damp basements he would grade the tobacco when we were working it off for market. However, Marshall didn't smoke or chew tobacco. He worked in the crop for an hourly wage.

One late summer afternoon when Marshall was in the orchard mowing grass along the creek bank with a scythe, a violent wind storm came up. I was with Aunt Bess, who cared for everyone and was anxious about the cattle, the chickens, the many farm buildings, the crops, as well as the people in a storm. I was glad she wasn't alone.

From the porch Aunt Bess and I saw Marshall making his way against the wind in the rain toward the house. Lightning cracked repeatedly and very close. Ozone hung heavy in the air. Thunder rumbled and tumbled all around us in the darkened afternoon downpour. We were in the center of the storm.

When Marshall made it onto the porch, he said, "By Ned, Bessie, when I seed them trees bow down to the wind, I started for the house, and when I came near the fence, that wind just lifted me off the ground, right up in the air, and I said, 'Lord, if it's yore will, it's fine with me,' and then, by Ned, that wind just let me down real easy like, that lightnin' just crackin' all around. I know it ain't my time yet to go."

"You all come on in the kitchen, off the porch," Aunt Bess said as she went inside.

But I loved to watch the storm. The creek between the house and the barn was turning muddy and rising. It would go over the cart bridge and the foot bridge to the outhouses. Also when lightning hit a tree on the mountain near a barbed-wire fence, the lightning would run the fence in a streak of red or blue down the hillside to the rail fence close to the barn or house. I didn't need an explanation of why the wire fences became plank or rail before they reached the barn lots.

While Marshall was retelling his story to me and Uncle Gaston who sat with the newspaper on the porch, Aunt Bess stuck her head out the door from the kitchen and said, "Marshall Gregg, if I didn't know you never touch whiskey, I'd say you were drunk. I wouldn't tell such a tale! Don't come in here because I don't want to be close to you when you're struck by lightning for such talk." Then she added for me, "Get away from Marshall, Joe Dicky, so you won't get struck too!"

Marshall laughed and said, "By Ned, Bessie, it's the truth."

It was a wonderful storm. When it was over, we could see that the cornfield, the big barn, the granary over the tobacco basement, and the orchard were in the line that the twister of strong wind cut through the farm. It laid the tall corn flat in a path wide as a road through the field. It lifted the two wide, high doors to the barn loft off their track and flung them to the ground in the lot toward the granary which it tipped off its foundation.

Marshall repeated his story many times for me and ended it by saying, "You see, Little Buddy, there's no need to be afraid, you won't go 'til your time comes."

But the time had not come for me to learn where Marshall went in his absence from the farm.

*   *   *

In August when the corn and tobacco crops were laid by, Marshall was absent from the farm again. Also each August, Zion Hill Baptist Church held a memorial day, a homecoming time with a program of all-day singing and dinner on the ground. The graveyard where generations of people were buried lay on the hillside next to the white clapboard church with its single belfry over the main entrance. The tombstones stood over the hillside even to the timberline. The red clay was scraped and shaped into mounds above each grave the week before Homecoming Sunday, and then each family brought baskets of flowers to decorate the graves. The hillside became a radiant flower garden, and on decoration day not everyone could get into the small church for the worship program, so many people visited together among the flowers and gravestones.

On one especially bright morning I helped Mother carry armloads of flowers up the hill to the Morgan grave plot. While she was arranging the jars and vases, I watched the crowds of people across the hillside. It was then I saw Marshall's bandanna. He was with Katy and her sisters, Connie and Sally. They had brought tubs of gladioli and had covered the entire family plot.

*   *   *

The years passed. I left the farm for military service.

Meanwhile, Marshall grew older and after Uncle Oliver was killed in a tractor accident Marshall, too, left the farm—his log cabin and flower garden abandoned to birds, opossum, raccoons, chipmunks, and rabbits. Cattle drank freely from his cool spring among the shade trees. Marshall, I learned, had moved to Brooks Branch.

It was during a visit home one summer that my mother said, "Joe, would you like to drive over to Brooks Branch this afternoon? We could visit some people you haven't seen for a long time."

It was a dry day, so Mother and I dared the dirt road and drove all the way up the cove over the ruts and rocks to Bud Brooks's house. When Mother stopped the car, she said, "Marshall lives here now with Katy and Bud." She gave me time to take it all in before she went on. "They're all in their late eighties. I check on them often since they're so far back in this cove without a phone."

We sat in the car a moment and looked around on the quiet clearing. Mother said, "They haven't heard the car. They're probably on the back porch. Why don't you go knock on the door?"

I didn't see anyone in the garden as I walked through the tall grass to the front door, but for some reason, I didn't knock. I walked around the end of the house toward the back facing the mountain. I didn't intend to eavesdrop but I stopped behind the large lilac bush at the corner when I heard hearty laughter.

I stood looking through the bush to see Katy rocking on the porch and laughing as she watched Marshall sitting in a straight chair with a white barber's towel spread around him with lather all over his face, chin, and neck. Marshall and Bud were laughing too.

Bud was stropping a straight razor on a long flat leather strap hanging on a porch post. In his laughter, he wiped a moist eye on his sleeve and said to Marshall, "I ain't as steady as I used to be. So stop your chucklin' afore the lather dries or I might nip your throat."

I stood and watched Bud begin to shave Marshall, the straight razor held steady, and with deft strokes, he gave Marshall a perfect shave, not a single nick in his thin and tender skin. Mother, as usual, had brought a bag of peaches and a cantaloupe for them. We didn't stay long.

* * *

Some years later on a trip home to the mountains to visit Mother in Asheville's Aston Park Hospital, I saw Marshall for the last time. While with Mother in her room, I heard from down the hallway "By Ned, lassie, I don't need no more medicine."

"That's got to be Marshall Gregg!" I said to Mother.

"Yes, Marshall's here; you must go see him. He has pneumonia. The nurses say he's a real case—won't wear any of the hospital gowns. See if he remembers you."

I went down the hall to his room and looked in. It was a ward with three other men in the large room, windows open wide onto the hot summer street. Marshall lay naked under the thin white sheet, his slender handsome body belying his ninety-four years. I stood quietly beside his bed.

Marshall cocked his head on his high pillow and looked up at me.

"Hello, Marshall," I said. "Do you remember me?"

He studied my face awhile, then his eyes lit up and he grinned, "By Ned! You're Buddy Morgan's boy. You've come to see your mother. I knowed she's here."

Neither his memory nor his sight were diminished by the passing years. We talked a bit about the good old days before Marshall said, "By Ned, I'm going home soon." He rested a moment and then added, "To my 'long home,' as old Preacher Collins used to say."

I held his hand in both of mine and said, "Good-bye, Marshall." We both knew his time had come.

Anner

I heard the church bell tolling as snow flurries whirled around me and the team. I gripped the handles of the bull-tongue plow and watched the upturned soil slide off the wing of the steel blade. Big snow flakes rested a second on the slick soil before vanishing forever. The large white flakes lay longer on the plow tongue, but on the warm, dark hips of the two mules they melted immediately. It was a January morning and I was winter plowing—slowly turning furrow after furrow across the bottomland. Dad and I had been taking turns behind the plow for a few days. Acres of upturned soil lay in smooth, rolling mounds on my left toward the creek.

The team and I plowed toward the line fence that marked the beginning of Mr. Mark Daves's farm. In the distance, billows of gray smoke from the chimneys of the Daves home mingled with the snow cloud in the dark gray sky over the valley. The shadowy silhouette of their weathered, gray clapboard house swam somewhere between earth and heaven in the gathering mist.

I knew that Miss Anner lay ill there on her bed near the open fireplace. Since before Christmas Mother had been helping Ellie keep Anner clean, bringing sheets and clothes to our house to wash. I had watched Anner lie still on her pillow, not bothering to wave a fly from her forehead. I had watched Ellie, her sister, brush out her long gray hair and wrap it into its bun on top of Anner's head, and I had seen Anner lie in bed with her long gray hair let down. The smell of camphor and bedpan came to me.

Each evening lately I had seen Doctor Reeves's dove-gray Studebaker coupe ford the creek and crawl slowly up the drive into their yard. Two giant maples towered over the house leafless and still.

As I watched the patterns in the upturned earth, the tolling of the church bell drifted lightly on the wind—an even series of *dong . . . dong . . . dong.* I wasn't counting tolls, just guiding the plow and watching the soil turn upside down in one continuous furrow. Old Tom walked in the open furrow while Kate kept pace on the stubble land. The team, the plow, and I were leaving no trace of last year's crop.

Out of the corner of my eye, I became aware of a man's silhouette walking in Dad's manner across the plowed field at an angle to conjunct with me and the team near the line fence. I had not been plowing long enough for him to relieve me at the plow or for him to bring me a morning snack. As he walked he rested his empty hands inside his overalls' bib.

The mules stopped as Dad approached.

"Put the team away and come on to the house," he said quietly.

"It's not too wet to plow," I protested, "and the ground's not frozen."

He looked kindly at me from his light blue eyes and said, "You hear the church bell? Anner's dead. Amos went to toll the bell. Mark and Ellie'll need us. Your mother went over to help lay her out. When you get to the other end of the field, take the plow to the shed. Get a move on." He turned toward home.

I heard the somber bell begin again. As the team and I made our way to the barn, I counted eighty-two tolls. "So Anner was eighty-two years old," I thought to myself, for Dad had told me once that Amos tolled the bell once for each year of the person who had died. It was late January. Mother was then pregnant with my brother who was born in April that year.

Nevertheless, I found Mother standing beside Ellie at Anner's bedside. Ellie sat in a straight chair and wept quietly, her hands over her face. Anner's body lay straight, her hands on her chest under the neatly folded quilt edge. The pennies on her eyelids, the relaxed mouth, and the bloodless, white face were certain clues of death, but somehow the pain was washed from her brow.

I heard Mother say, "Anner's suffering is over, Ellie. She's at rest."

But Ellie cried, "Sister, Sister! Deller, she's gone forever, ain't it!"

Mr. Mark, their brother, stood by the window watching for the undertakers to come up the drive. Tears rolled down his cheeks when he looked toward Ellie whose open grief seemed inconsolable.

The snow had turned to a fine mist and the sun had come out from behind the gray clouds. The room was clean and bright in contrast to the human sadness. Anner in death lay still in the center of the iron bed under the colorful patchwork quilt made by her own hands. The window shades were raised and light flooded the room through lace curtains. Against the papered walls over Anner's bed, the Daveses' father and mother watched sternly from their almost life-sized images framed in mahogany. Ellie's cot, from where she cared for Anner in the night and kept the fire going, had been folded up and stood against the mantle in Mr. Mark's bedroom. Bottles of medicine and snuff tins stood on the mantle over the fireplace in the living room. The large rocking chair and a knitting rocker flanked the hearth. Several caned straight chairs stood against the walls but everyone except Ellie and Mother, who had sat down beside her, remained standing.

The gray Cadillac hearse from Dunn and Gross Funeral Home purred slowly up the drive and then backed to the edge of the porch between the main house and the kitchen wing. No dogs barked.

Mr. Mark stepped out the door and met the two younger men as they opened the rear door of the hearse and began to remove a stretcher-bed. They swung it onto the porch and snapped the wheels down in place.

I stood silent on the hearth from where I could see the men follow Mr. Mark into the room, one at each end of the slender chrome bed on high wheels. Ellie stood quietly by Anner's bed wringing her hands held close to her breasts. Tears flowed down her cheeks.

When the undertakers stopped the stretcher near the bed, Ellie doubled over and wailed, "I can't stand it! Don't take her yet." Mother, weeping openly, closed her arms around Ellie to steady her. Then Mr. Mark turned her from Mother and held her shoulders and shook her firmly.

"Ellie, don't make no scene," he scolded. "Come out

here with me to the dining room," he said as he held her wrist and guided her into the next room toward the kitchen wing of the house. I could see him place his arm around her, and they put their heads together while Mr. Mark talked to her, his left hand slicing the air in sharp gestures. No one could hear what he was saying.

Meanwhile, Anner's body was laid on the stretcher bed, rolled onto the porch, and placed in the hearse. The door was closed on the car.

* * *

The little fenced Daves family graveyard lay in the shade of ancient oaks to the east and north sides. One giant oak shaded it from the western sun, but a person had a panoramic view of the Daves farm and of the entire valley west and south from the plot. In summer, dairy and beef cattle grazed nearby or lay chewing their cud in the shade. Mr. Mark kept the cemetery grass mowed and the tombstones in place. Early graves were marked only by a single slab of rock set endwise in the earth. Names and dates had long ago worn away. One grave had a metal funeral home marker standing with the ink inscription faded beneath the clear plastic, but the Daveses' parents lay beneath a large double marble monument. Before he left, Mr. Mark showed us where to dig Anner's grave.

Uncle Oliver, Amos, Marshall, my father, and I stayed to dig Anner's grave. Amos marked the grave's sides—three feet by six feet. "We'll dig six feet down," he assured us.

The picks and shovels and mattocks were put to work. The dirt was piled on one side only. One man worked the pick, then another shovelled out the loosened dirt. It was hard digging in the undisturbed clay. Only one man could work in the hole at once, but we passed the time talking and waiting a turn at the stubborn clay.

"'Member the time Mark and them women was robbed?" Marshall asked.

"Yeah," said Dad, "they'd gone to church meeting when Lee Hamlet and Charlie Cole went into their house and took their money."

"How much do you s'pose they got?" asked Marshall. "Since the depression Mark never trusted no bank."

"It was just egg money and such that Anner kept, I think," said Dad. "Each of them kept their own money separate."

"Why?" asked Amos.

"Mark told me," my dad began, "that he and Ellie wanted to build a new house, but Anner said they didn't need another house and none of her money was going into another house, so she began to keep her money separate."

"I bet they've got pots full of cash hidden away," mumbled Marshall.

"Got what?" asked my Uncle Oliver who was hard of hearing.

"Pots of gold!" Marshall shouted.

Uncle Oliver laughed.

My father took a more reasonable view of the Daveses' money. "A few eggs and butter to market each week and a small tobacco crop each year is not enough to live on, much less to hoard." He added, "It takes a lot just to buy grain for Mark's horses."

"By Ned, now them's beautiful horses!" Marshall put

in. "And Mark don't work 'em none too hard."

Amos climbed out of the grave hole and Marshall took a turn with the shovel. I was reminded of a time a year or so before, and I asked, "Dad, do you remember the evening you sent me to see what was wrong with Mr. Mark's horses?"

"Yeah," he answered slowly.

"What was wrong?" asked Amos.

"Well, it was a nice summer evening after supper when I looked over and saw Anner and Ellie pulling the cultivator with Mark guiding it between the bean rows in the garden. Mark had been working the horses all day disking the wheat stubble and I thought maybe the horses had got down or something, so I sent Joe over to see if they'd like a mule to pull the cultivator.

"What'd they say when you got there?" Dad asked me.

I remembered that I had run over in my bare feet and up into the garden. "They were resting a bit when I got there, and I said, 'Dad sent me to see what's wrong with your horses.' Miss Anner said, 'They're resting. They've had a hard day and me and Ellie can pull this cultivator through these few rows of beans.'

"There was nothing wrong with the horses," I continued. "Mr. Mark said, 'It was easier to just let Anner and Ellie pull the plow than to harness up a horse for such a few rows.' I thought it was all Anner's idea."

"Yeah, I guess it was," Dad said. "Anner was the boss. She was twenty when Mark was born and she raised him, and she's always been the boss."

"They'll miss her," Amos said.

118

As the grave grew deeper, the man climbing out reached the shovel handle up to another on the ground who held the handle firmly while the digger walked up the clay wall holding on to the other end of the shovel. At last the grave was six feet deep, and the man working in the new hole could see only the sky because the banks were higher than his head.

Amos believed in neat side walls and he climbed down with the spade to trim the lower walls. "Give Miss Anner a good grave. She'll be in it a long time." he said.

I jumped down and threw out the last shovelfuls of loose dirt, and Dad gave me his hand and pulled me up out of Anner's new grave.

It was winter on the ridge but I don't remember being cold. The work and the company kept me warm.

* * *

Mother and other neighbor women helped Ellie clean and get ready for the wake. They baked and cooked and took lots of food and left it on Ellie's dining table. Anner's bed was broken down and placed in Mark's bedroom alongside Ellie's cot.

When Anner's body was returned home the next day, the undertakers placed her coffin along the wall where her deathbed had stood. Flowers began to arrive even before the hearse did. Soon wreaths, vases, sprays, and baskets sur-rounded the casket and lined the wall. The undertakers left wire stands so the flowers were banked from the floor up to the level of the gray casket on all that wall.

Anner's casket was open. With her gray hair in a perfect bun on top of her head and dressed in a deep purple dress with a white collar, Anner looked very formal and peaceful. The spray of red roses on the foot of her casket had one wide, white ribbon across them which read "Beloved Sister."

It was the custom for neighbors to gather and to talk in the house during the wake and for a few people to sit and talk in the room with the corpse through most of the night.

In the wake of Anner's passing, a community stopped to mourn her death and to comfort Mark and Ellie. When their own chores were finished, friends and neighbors helped with the chores on Mr. Mark's farm.

There was much talk, but in the room with Anner's body the conversations were quiet. Everyone spoke first to Ellie who sat near the fire and then looked at Anner in her coffin. Then each one admired the flowers.

Even though there were snow showers during the evening, about everybody on Newfound came by to pay their respects. Eventually the crowd thinned and I noticed my father and Uncle Oliver were able to get Mr. Mark alone at the end of the dining table. I overheard a few comments and understood why Dad and Mother had stayed late.

"Mark, Anner's doctor bills and all must have been a good amount," my Uncle Oliver began. "And Dunn and Gross Funeral Home services cost. Buddy and I want to help pay the bills if you need some help."

"Oliver, that's mighty kind," Mr. Mark drawled, "but it's all paid. Anner had enough laid by to cover the costs. She's paid her own way."

"Well, just holler if you need anything. You know we're ready to help," my father added.

Mr. Mark took out his handkerchief and blew his nose

loudly and dried his eyes. Dad said to me, "Get your mother and let's go home. Mark and Ellie's cousins will stay to-night. They won't be alone."

On the way home I asked my father whether the Daves-es might have any insurance. He looked at me a moment and then said, "Son, they don't need no insurance. They've got neighbors."

Mrs. Pearl Robertson and Her Car

"Oh, no, not right now!" I thought to myself as I saw Mr. and Mrs. Robert Robertson trudging up the slope of our lawn. I was standing on a scaffold painting under the overhang of the kitchen roof. White paint had run back on my hand from the brush and I was well covered with paint splatters. Certainly I would have to put the paint bucket away and scrub with turpentine before I could give Mrs. Robertson another driving lesson.

"The old woman thought we'd go to the store," Mr. Robertson said to me as I turned toward them. Mrs. Robertson was somewhat deaf, and Mr. Robertson always spoke softly. I don't think she heard much of what he said.

"I won't interrupt your work," Mrs. Robertson shouted. "I believe I can drive to the store and back OK. I'll keep it in low gear."

"Let me put this paint away and I can ride with you while you practice changing gears," I almost pleaded, for I didn't feel that any life was safe without me to grab the wheel while Mrs. Robertson changed gears.

When Mr. Robertson had retired from the Champion Paper and Fiber Company in Canton, he and his wife had bought the house in the hollow above our pasture and had moved from the city. Neither one had ever owned a car, nor had either ever driven one.

Mrs. Robertson was a tall, large, dominating woman.

Her husband, on the other hand, was short and thin and usually stood in his wife's shadow. One day Mrs. Robertson took it into her head that they needed a car and that she would learn to drive it. "So we can go to church and to the store without bothering anyone," she had explained.

The right-of-way to their house led up a clay road across our cow pasture. There were two gates, one at the public road and one at the line fence. Their drive was slick when wet; therefore Dad had said that until Mrs. Robertson learned to drive, she should keep her car in our yard. She did. It was parked right beside my basketball goal post.

Their son, William, refused absolutely to help her learn to drive, saying that when his parents wanted something, they could just ask him. But he worked a shift at the paper factory and wasn't always available.

The car Mrs. Robertson purchased was a sturdy, 1938 black Plymouth, three speed with a straight, six-cylinder engine that was strong as a tractor's. The body was well-kept, and of course, I loved to drive that car.

At first, I had driven Mrs. Robertson to town or to church, but for some weeks lately she had insisted on sitting behind the wheel. Simply put, she had not mastered the art of the smooth start, nor the art of smooth acceleration, nor the easy change of gears from first to second to third; nor had she reliable judgment of the space her automobile occupied on the road.

After she started the car, she disengaged the clutch, placed the transmission in low gear, revved up the engine until she could hear it humming, and let the clutch out suddenly. Starts were leaps and jumps until she gathered a feel for the correct gas feed.

Moving at full throttle in low gear, her change to second was an outright tempting of destiny. She took her eyes from the bright road and peered into the dark floorboard to locate the clutch with her left foot. She depressed it without letting her right foot ease up on the accelerator. The engine would whine as she shoved the gear lever from low up by reverse with a tremendous scraping to second and let the clutch spring out to engage while the engine was roaring.

In second, the car always gave a great leap forward as the power wheels dug gravel. Then Mrs. Robertson gave the accelerator a series of pumps. The car would leap and stall and leap and stall until she gained some feel for acceleration again. Weeks of lessons and practice had not made any improvement in her coordination or driving skill.

The Plymouth, however, seemed indestructible.

While I was in school, Mrs. Robertson would often practice her driving. At first, she practiced backing out of our yard. I returned home once to find her car abandoned in Mr. Mark's hayfield near the creek side. Dad said that she had gotten the car into reverse, shot over the gravel road, through the wire fence, and somehow killed the engine just before the car would have dropped into the creek. I drove it across the hayfield to Mr. Mark's driveway and back to its parking space at my basketball hoop.

Another evening, I stepped off the school bus and saw that the Plymouth was not in our yard. "Mom, where is Mrs. Robertson and her car?" I asked.

"As a matter of fact," she answered, "the car's in the ditch near Uncle Taylor's barn, and Mrs. Robertson is at home fixing dinner."

I had run up the road to assess the damages on the car, but there were none. Uncle Taylor told me that Mrs. Robertson just climbed out after she plowed into the ditch and said that Joe would drive it back to Buddy's yard. She had been trying to change to second gear and had taken her eyes off the road in the curve. The car had stalled against the ditch side within twenty feet of a spill into the deep, open branch below the culvert.

Dad hooked a chain to the car and pulled it back onto the road with the tractor. I drove it home.

* * *

It was near noon as I climbed back onto the scaffold. The Robertsons had decided that my instruction would not be needed on this short drive to the store only one mile away.

"I'll keep it in low gear all the way to the store and all the way back," Mrs. Robertson promised loudly as she marched to her car.

Little traffic used the road, especially around noontime. However, there was one tryst between a man and woman who met on the mountain road during their lunch hours. The man drove his truck by our house, up the mountain road and stopped in the deep inside curve. A few minutes later each day, a lady in a new, red Mercury would also drive up the mountain road and park next to the truck in the cool shade high above the valley. The Mercury always went by trailing a tunnel of dust.

The man passed our house in his truck on his way to the mountain rendezvous before Mrs. Robertson started her car. After Mr. Robertson got in beside his wife, there was the usual roar of the engine, the quick grab of the indomitable clutch, the leap forward, and they were off.

I listened as the engine whined in low gear, the sound fading as the car left my sight. She was driving slowly. I could imagine her gripping the steering wheel with both hands and peering straight ahead, her foot unsteady on the accelerator.

Down the valley, the road runs straight from our house to a blind, left curve at the bottom of the graveyard hill. Most drivers tooted their car horns in the daylight upon approaching the curve, as the road was narrow.

On the scaffold again, I had dipped my brush back into the paint and had resumed my work when I heard the Mercury's sharp horn sound beyond the blind bend. Instantly, I realized that the lady was later than usual, that she was driving faster than usual, and that Mrs. Robertson was approaching the curve too.

Then I heard the fence wires pulling from both directions, and snapping and popping and breaking. I heard a tremendous crash that echoed against the mountains.

I jumped from the scaffold with the paint brush still in my hand and ran into the road. I saw only the underside of the Robertson's Plymouth, for it was lying on its right side below the road in the curve, the black tires still turning. I stood transfixed and stared at the incredible.

It was my Uncle Taylor's car sliding to a stop on the gravel behind me that brought me to action. Uncle Taylor was white with fear of the worst. "Get in, Joe," he yelled at me. "Mrs. Robertson's killed herself this time!" He had been sitting on his porch and had seen the accident happen.

We stopped in the curve. Mr. Mark had run over from his house and was looking into the windshield of the Plymouth. The new red Mercury had stopped near the inside bank of the curve—no sign of collision.

The Plymouth lay on its side, no evidence of any real damage to it. It was clear that Mrs. Robertson had steered too close to the outer edge of the road and the soft shoulder on the bank had given way, but the wire fence had caught the car and then dropped it on its side below the road in the hayfield.

The Mercury lady was standing in the center of the road with one hand over her mouth. "Oh, God!" she said.

Uncle Taylor and I rushed to the Plymouth, and I opened up the driver's door, one that opened from front to back. I stood on the car's side to hold the door open. It took all three of us men to help Mrs. Robertson climb out onto the side of the hood and over the headlights to the ground. We turned to help Mr. Robertson who by then had stood up and put his head out the door opening.

"Are you hurt, Bob?" Uncle Taylor inquired.

Mr. Robertson said calmly, "The old woman fell on me!"

Mr. Mark

"I don't think Mark is hoeing his tobacco. It looks like he's chopping it down," my father mused as we looked across the field. Then he said to me, "You don't suppose he's gone off his rocker, do you?"

We were leaving our cow barn after milking, but Dad had stopped in his tracks to watch Mr. Mark's strange behavior. Tobacco was Mr. Mark's money crop. Most farmers had a dairy or some beef cattle and a small tobacco patch, but Mr. Mark's income depended on his acre allotment of tobacco and a few Hereford cattle that he pastured on the mountain.

Early in February, like everyone else, Mr. Mark had burned a tobacco bed up next to his orchard. The familiar white canvas had been spread over the straw on the bed after he sowed the almost invisible, but expensive, seeds. Then he had deep-plowed the acre between his big barn and his tool sheds. He had disked the soil and laid off the rows four feet apart.

When the plants were eight inches high in the bed, he had transplanted them to his field. Ellie had helped him for a week of backbreaking hand labor, pulling the plants from the bed, carrying them to the field, and planting and watering them one at a time.

Later he had replanted any spots where the original shoots had failed to take roots. He and Ellie had hoed the weeds out, and he had side-dressed the crop with nitrogen. At last it was June, and his tobacco field was turning a rich green. He always had healthy tobacco that developed wide, yellow leaves by late August.

"After all that work, why is he chopping it down?" my father asked. "The man must be crazy," he muttered.

"Maybe it's got some disease," I suggested.

"There's nothing wrong with the tobacco," Dad said ironically. At the supper table, Father was unusually quiet.

"Cat got your tongue?" Mother asked.

"It's Mark, Della," Dad explained. "He's chopping down his tobacco with his hoe. He cut down eight or so rows after he and Ellie got through their chores."

Mother didn't seem disturbed at all. "I'm sure he has a good reason," she said.

"Oh, shitfire! You don't know what's come over the man, Della!" Dad exploded. "He's had that bunion the size of a golf ball on the side of his head for years. It's got to affect his mind sometime."

"There's some explanation," Mother said calmly.

"Of course, there's *some* explanation. Why the man's crazy!" my father argued.

"I saw the county farm agent's car there the other day," Mother began.

"That don't make no difference!" my father interrupted. "He was just surveying to see that Mark has only an acre planted and, of course, he does. He measured it himself."

Mother still spoke calmly. "Maybe he made a mistake. Maybe his patch is larger than an acre and the government has . . ."

"Della! Something is wrong with the man!" Dad interrupted.

"Maybe the government has cut his allotment," Mother finished her thought.

After a few minutes of silence, Dad said quietly, "I just can't believe that all is well over there."

*　*　*

Mr. Mark had taken a very bad fall some months after Anner died. Getting Anner's casket to the Daves family cemetery on the ridge had been a tedious business, but Mark's taking her tombstone up there on the sled pulled by one of his big Clydesdale horses had ended in accident.

The hearse with Anner's casket had crawled up the clay drive that entered Dad's pasture and curved by our cow barn. It was necessary to climb the steep drive up the hill to the woods and then drive around the hillside along the timberline out to the cemetery on the ridge.

Tractors were the only motor vehicles that I had ever seen circle the hill. However, the hearse made its way along the edge of the woods on snow-covered grass. When the driver reached the place where the ridge slanted down toward the cemetery, he stopped, for the slant of the hillside grew critical and fell steeply toward the valley below. On the snow and ice the hearse might slide sideways.

My cousin, Don, told the driver to wait and he would get his bulldozer. He attached a logging chain to the back frame of the hearse to hold it steady. The sleek, gray Cadillac had appeared to be pulling the bulldozer as the two vehicles edged down the ridge.

When the stonecutters delivered Anner's marble monument to Ellie and Mark, the driver was afraid to drive his truck onto the ridge. It was a bright, summer day when Mr. Mark took his strong mare and dragged the heavy stone on his sled to the graveyard.

As he and the horse and sled came back off the hill and by our cow barn, I went out to open the gate for him. The grassy, clay drive led along a high bank above the public, gravel road to the gate. Mr. Mark was standing on his sled holding the reins in one hand loosely, trusting his horse completely when a car whizzed by on the road below.

The mare shied and jumped, jerking the sled from under Mark's feet. He fell backwards like a tree trunk off the sled onto the grass and rolled like a log under the barbed-wire fence, down the steep bank, through the bramble and briars and landed in the ditch beside the public road. The mare lunged through the open gate and dragged the sled home behind her.

Mr. Mark picked himself up, staggered a moment, and said, "Well, I'll be! Wonder who that was that went by in that car like that?"

Dad had rushed out from the barn and asked, "Are you all right, Mark?"

"I reckon so," was all he said, but he had had a very bad fall.

* * *

Dad and I walked over rows of wilted tobacco plants, cut down and dug up and left to rot in the sun. Mr. Mark was destroying the crop slowly and methodically, just as he had always worked.

When we approached, he stopped chopping, placed his

right hand on the top of his hoe handle, then placed his left armpit over his hand and leaned on his hoe. He grinned at Dad. "Where's your hoe, Buddy?"

Dad was not prepared to take a flippant view of the matter. He asked gingerly, "Don't you reckon you've cut your patch down small enough all ready?"

"Oh, I'm not through yet, Buddy," he drawled.

Dad stood speechless waiting for further information.

"It seems like a great waste of a good crop," I said. Dad gave me a quick piercing look that meant "Keep your mouth shut."

Mr. Mark laughed and said, "Yeah, Joe Boy, it is that." We waited.

Finally, Mr. Mark said, "The farm agent brought out a government man t'other day, Buddy."

"Yeah?" my father urged.

"He made me what he called 'a proposition.'"

We stood in the center of the tobacco patch, and Mr. Mark looked around himself at his own handiwork.

"What do you mean, 'a proposition,' Mark?" Dad asked quietly.

"I talked it over with Ellie," he began. "She thought of all the work yet to do to get the stuff to market. Sucker it ever' week and top it." Mr. Mark looked at the mountaintops. "Iffin it didn't hail on it when it's ripe, it'd be in the August heat when we'd have to cut it, and spud it, and lug it onto the sled, and hang it in the barn."

"Yeah," Dad said patiently.

"Then in November, in the cold, we'd have to catch it in case to work it off."

"Oh, law me, yes," Dad said and he swallowed a lump in his throat.

"Then there's the gamble at the market. The prices might be down. The agent said there's a good chance the price'd be down."

Dad asked again, "What was the proposition, Mark?"

"That government man said they'd pay me *not* to grow any tobacco this year."

Dad stared at him with his mouth open.

"They put my allotment into what he called a 'land bank.' So I signed the papers, and I get my money for leaving the land fallow. What do you think of that, Buddy?"

"It sounds like a wise thing you've done," my father conceded.

Mr. Mark watched Dad's face a moment and laughed as he said, "Well, I ain't crazy."

LOVER

Corn Shucking

I was chopping large, orange pumpkins into bite-sized pieces to feed the dairy cows when I looked up to see two cars pull into the yard. Dad had walked out from the dairy to get a bucket of pumpkin chunks to pour into the manger.

"Looks like the neighbors are going to slip on the corn tonight," he muttered as he stood beside me watching the cars unload. And then we noticed Marshall and Bud and Uncle Oliver and Aunt Carrie walking through the low, winter rye toward the house. Another car parked on the grass beside the plank fence near the old hollyhocks.

Suddenly, my heart leaped when I heard Shirley laughing. My close friend, Don Rogers, had driven up in his '39 Chevy with Shirley and several of our school friends. I couldn't explain it then, but I felt somehow that I'd remember that evening.

"Where'd you pile that corn, Buddy?" someone asked as the men began to gather around us and the pumpkins. The women, carrying dishes of food, walked toward the kitchen door where Aunt Bess stood laughing and greeting each one with a fond hug. There would be a big, late supper when the corn was shucked out.

* * *

It was late October. For the past two weeks Dad had been gathering corn. It had had to be done when the weather was dry and one could get the team and wagon into the fields. Each afternoon as soon as I stepped off the school bus I had heard Dad call, "Hey, Joe! Get over here quick!" Since his motto for me was "quick as the word," I changed my clothes and ran to the field where he was working. Dad and I pulled each ear from its stalk and tossed it onto the wagon load. Basketball coach Conley Rogers had once said to me after he witnessed one of my lucky shots, "I find you boys who chop wood and pitch corn are pretty accurate with your hands." We were.

Some mountain farmers walked through their fields pulling corn and tossing it into piles along the rows, then they returned later with their teams and wagons to pick it up, but Dad was an efficiency expert. He didn't believe in any extra lifting, so as he pulled each ear of corn he tossed it directly into the wagon. It was the same with his tools. He said, "While you have it in your hands, put it away properly."

Of course, one had to have a well-trained team of mules for the job. Tom and Kate were such a team. Dad would talk them through the fields. After he left the wagon to pull corn, he never touched the reins that hung on the wagon post. The mules responded to the "click, click" of his tongue and pulled the wagon forward. "Whoa" was all he needed to say for them to stop and wait for us to pull more corn.

We worked with gloved hands. I grasped the stalk just above the ear with one hand and with the other I grasped the ear of corn and twisted the husk as I ripped it from the stalk. Ungloved hands could be cut easily by slits of sharp stalk or husk. There were always two large ears per stalk of corn. Dad and I had thinned the corn back in the spring so that it yielded a hundred and fifty bushels to the acre.

When the corn was piled high above the sideboards, the mules heaved the heavy, groaning wagon out of the soft bottomland, forded the big creek, pulled it up the gravel drive by the house and forded the branch, rolled under the giant Bellflower apple trees, then wound above the cherry orchard and beyond the large hen house where we emptied the wagonloads of corn onto the deep orchard grass. Finally, the corn pile stood over four feet high and stretched for at least thirty feet over the grass.

After the corn was harvested, we returned the wagon back to the fields and drove through them picking up several loads of pumpkins which we unloaded at the end of the dairy barn. As I worked, I thought of all the pumpkin pies the women would bring and the fresh cream Aunt Bess would whip for the corn shuckers' dinner.

* * *

The Dills family arrived. Mr. Dills was one of Uncle Oliver's tenant farmers with a large family of boys. Jim Dills came with his girl, Helen Ward. They were in my class at school. Sam, the oldest, had joined the Navy. John Henry, the youngest son, had gotten his name from the doctor who delivered him. When the physician told Mrs. Dills, "It's a boy. What shall we name him?" Mrs. Dills had so wanted a girl that she said, "I don't care." "How about John Henry?" the doctor asked, and Mrs. Dills said simply, "Sounds OK." Like his namesake, John Henry was a strong, sharp, formidable young man. Only a stupid bully would tangle with him. And then only once.

But finally Mrs. Dills had given birth to a daughter.

Laura Bell, the youngest, was a lovely, blue-eyed, bashful girl four years younger than I. They all went directly to the corn pile.

I rather liked Laura Bell. As Jim, her brother, and I were good friends, we all often played together and sometimes were together in the fields hoeing corn or cutting tobacco. Also we sometimes walked to Sunday school together.

Shirley and I were the same age—classmates since first grade. Since I was the tallest boy and she the tallest girl in class, we had always been paired together by our teachers until many friends assumed that we were "made for each other." Any interest I might have in another girl had to be weighed in the balance of how I might hurt Shirley.

My evening was being complicated.

As is the custom at Christmas for the male to steal a kiss from the lady standing under the mistletoe, so at corn shucking the man who shucked a red ear of corn got to kiss the lady of his choice "then and there."

"What if I accidentally shuck a red ear?" I wondered. I hadn't had any experience in kissing. Well, almost none. I remembered playing Spin the Bottle at one of Ruth Ann's birthday parties and the bottle pointed at me once when Daphne Brown was in the hall waiting for her kiss.

Amid the cheers and whistles I entered the dark hall. Before the door was closed on Daphne and me, I saw where she stood looking so lovely and delicate. In the dark I took her shoulders in my hands and bent forward to plant my lips on hers, but my lips landed near her ear as she had turned her head to give me a cheek. I didn't know quite what to do next. Would she think I couldn't kiss if I quit here? I wondered. So while I held her shoulders firmly, I sort of chewed my way along her jaw until I found her lips, but not knowing quite what to do when I got there, I just quit sucking on her face, and turned her loose to return to the circle. Someone opened the door. Daphne escaped, and I waited for the next unfortunate girl to come into the kissing parlor. I pecked her on the cheek and got it over with.

Daphne never mentioned my kiss and certainly I never confessed my failure. I don't remember that Daphne ever looked directly at me again. Our encounter in the dark world would be our secret. I really didn't know how to do that sexy thing that everyone but me in the whole universe knew by instinct. I thought that maybe I'd be lucky and not find a red ear.

However, it was not to be.

By the time I drove the milked cows out of the barn, washed down the milking parlor, washed up the milk room, loaded the milk cans into the cooler, climbed the silo and tossed down the silage and then spread it down the manger of the lounging barn, and joined the people at the corn, one side of the long pile was lined with neighbors and friends laughing, talking, shucking, and pitching clean white ears across the unshucked corn.

Even though there was a bright, full moon, Uncle Taylor had hung a lantern on the corner of the log building where he kept the bull. The big Holstein stood quietly watching the shuckers through the gaps of his log stall. Also Dad had placed a lantern on the corn pile at the far end from the bull pen.

As they worked, some men sat on milking stools while others knelt on pads of folded toe-sacks. Women and young people stood. Many used homemade hand corn shuckers. Dad had made one for me. It was simply a wooden spike about five inches long whittled to a point at one end. Held in the left hand by two leather straps over the middle and little fingers, it could penetrate a husk with the point.

Each person reached for an ear, pulled the silk from the tip and ripped the husk down its length to expose the hard white corn inside, stripped away the other half of the shuck, broke the husk from the base of the ear, dropped the shuck behind him, and tossed the ear over onto the growing pile of clean corn. Shuckers developed a rhythm: bend-pick, rip-rip, break-toss; bend-pick, rip-rip, break-toss; bend-pick, rip-rip, break-toss. One broke his rhythm only to push the shucks away from his backside. At one of his breaks Uncle Taylor slipped a handful of husk into the pen for his bull.

I waded through the shucks behind the workers and noticed that someone had carved a face in a pumpkin, lit a candle in it, and placed the jack-o-lantern on a fence post out in the darkest shadow of an ancient apple tree.

I squeezed in between my friends Don and Bud Bonnom, careful not to choose either the side of Shirley or Laura Bell. To my left Shirley was shucking beside Jimmy at the end of the pile next to the bull pen while Laura Bell and her mother were on my right several paces down. Beside Bud Bonnom who was on my immediate right, Marshall sat on a stool shucking and listening to the talk. Beside Marshall, Uncle Gaston sat in a cane-bottomed, straight chair he had brought from the porch. He selected each ear with care, slowly pulled each husk, then brushed away any dry silk before he tossed the large ear butt first so that no grains might be cracked off upon impact. He would shuck one ear to Marshall's three.

"By Ned, I thought you'd get here soon, little Buddy," I heard Marshall say. "You can do some sparkin' tonight if you find a red ear." I noted the glint of mischief in his blue eyes.

In his usual way of exaggerating a word in every sentence, Don said, "Your Aunt Ruby just got a red ear and she *kissed* R. D. Now that *was* exciting." Uncle R. D. and Ruby were married and had three boys.

I hadn't shucked three ears before an unshucked ear of corn fell right in front of me. Out of the corner of my eye I saw that it came from Marshall's hand. I pretended to ignore it, but kept it at my feet so I wouldn't pick it up by accident.

When I glanced at Marshall, he was shucking and watching me out of the corner of his eye. He grinned and winked at me. So he knew that I knew he had planted a red ear for me to shuck. I decided to slip it over to Don when he turned to push his shucks away.

Perhaps someone planted the next red ear I discovered, but as I opened the husk and saw the red tip of the Indian corn, I dropped it, husk and all, and reached for another from the pile. So I had two red ears at my feet. Also I heard Marshall chuckling.

Bud, at my right, turned to push his shucks back and I laid one of the red ears over on his side. However, when he turned around, he picked it up and tossed it back in front of me and then laughed his bubbling "Hee!, Hee!, Hee!" I gave up hope of tricking one of those old men.

We kept shucking. R. D. got a red ear and kissed Aunt Ruby again. Dad got a red ear and said he'd save his kiss for Mother for later. The moon grew brighter and the corn pile grew smaller.

Finally, Bud, who was quite deaf and had a high-pitched voice, said very loudly, "Better shuck them ears at your feet. Hee! Hee! Hee!"

I kicked the red ears up closer to the big pile and one tumbled over in front of Don. He picked it up and shucked it. "Oh, *my gosh!*" he exclaimed as he held it up in the moonlight.

"You gotta choose a girl, Don," someone called out. Don had no particular girlfriend, and even in the dark I saw his ears glow red. His face flushed crimson at any focus of attention on him.

"Don, you've got a wide selection of girls!" my mother teased him quietly. There were my sisters Dot and Dean, Ruth Anne, Shirley, and Laura Bell to mention a few. Of course Helen was there with Jim, but she was taken.

Don said, "Eenie, Meenie, Miney, Mo; I think I'll kiss Laura Bell," and he turned toward her end of the line of shuckers. Laura Bell threw the ear she was shucking to the ground and hid behind her mother.

"Nobody ain't gonna kiss me," she said.

Mrs. Dills laughed and said, "You'll have to catch her first."

Mr. Dills added, "She's a mighty fast runner."

Don didn't chase her. His face turned another shade of

blush red and he said, "I'll just save my kiss for someone later."

Then I decided to shuck the red ear and choose Shirley. Aunt Bess arrived then. She took a place beside Uncle Taylor and said to everybody, "You all come to the house now and let's eat."

Uncle Taylor seconded her. "You've been a mighty help, people," he began. "Buddy and me can finish this corn tomorrow. It won't take no time." There were about three hundred bushels shucked and perhaps fifty more to go.

"Yes, much obliged," Dad added.

People got to their feet, surveyed their work, and began to stroll through the orchard toward the foot bridge and on to the house.

Uncle Taylor and Dad took down their lanterns. I showed Aunt Bess my ear of red corn, and she said, "I'll trade you that red ear for two pieces of pumpkin pie with fresh whipped cream."

That was a deal I couldn't resist.

Dad's Model-A Ford

Always before Dad gave me the keys to the A-Model he questioned me: "Can you remember to park the car in the shade? Not under a sap-dripping tree? Park on an incline so you can coast off and catch the engine and save the battery? Can you drive sensibly, not show off and kill somebody? Remember the Ford is old? Don't depend too much on them mechanical brakes? Don't let anyone else drive the car? Don't overload the car? No riding on the running boards? Don't fold down the top? It's old and brittle. Can you behave yourself and watch out for others?"

Usually I answered, "Yes, yes, yes," and thanked him when he handed over the keys, but that evening before he finished his routine questions I snapped, "Do I have to listen to all that stuff again? I'm late for my date." I held out my hand.

"Then you can do without the car," he said firmly and put the keys back into his pocket. He turned from me, sat down in his rocking chair, and picked up his paper.

I turned to Mother who was washing dishes at the sink.

"I heard," she said. "It's your father's car, not yours, and if you can't be patient enough to listen to his instructions, you don't deserve to get it."

"Shirley will be waiting," I whined. "What will I do?" We had no telephone. Shirley lived over four miles away, but we couldn't walk the eight miles from her house to the high school anyway.

* * *

Dad's 1928 Model-A was well over twenty years old before I got my driver's license. It was not unusual when in town to find men standing around the parked car, admiring it and asking "Is it for sale?" One of the first Fords to have mechanical brakes, Dad's convertible had a rumble seat for two. The glass windbreakers on each side of the windshield glistened like clean rimless spectacles. The black pinstripes on the gray-blue body matched its black fenders. Chrome, double-spring bumpers gleamed along with the small chrome hubcaps on the large, blue, spoked wheels. The spare tire mounted on a fifth rim hung on the rear behind the rumble seat.

Inside, the gear lever and the parking brake lever stood in the center of the floorboard under the dashboard. The switch bumped out in the "on" position on the chrome meter panel. In addition to the gas pedal on the floorboard there was a hand throttle on the steering wheel column and a hand gauge for the spark. At high speeds (from thirty to forty miles per hour) one "gave it more spark."

The Model-A had no glove compartment, but the removable front seat covered a large tool bin for inner tube repair kits, extra boots for tires, a jack, a hand air pump, an air pressure gauge, lug wrenches, and other necessary tools. In winter Dad installed the isinglass curtains, and he always drained the radiator when garaging the car.

Mother had learned to drive on the Model-A while my parents were courting. As a boy, I sat on Dad's lap behind the wheel and learned to steer. When I was tall enough to reach the controls, Dad gave me the driver's seat.

I was just twelve when he let me drive it alone. My friend Jimmy Robertson and I wanted to see a movie in Asheville. I drove the Model-A down the Old Leicester Highway to the County Farm, the old folks' home, then I took the gravel road over Dryman's Mountain, drove on down through Emma and up Florida Avenue behind the Dixie Home Supermarket in West Asheville. I parked the A-Model, and we walked out front of the market to Haywood Road and caught the city bus to Asheville.

Dad said, "Use your head. Don't drive in town or you'll be locked up." At twelve I had enough sense to listen to his advice.

Once, before I had my license, I wanted to go to the show in Asheville with Jim Dills and Jimmy Robertson. A spring flood had washed out the bridge over Newfound Creek, leaving drivers on Morgan Branch only one way out—over the Hutchinson mountain and down Turkey Creek to Leicester Highway.

At first Dad had said no to us because the rains had also left the mountain road awash in slick, red clay. Cars had churned the clay roadbed into deep, slick ruts up the first steep incline at the foot of the mountain road. Many drivers had taken runs at the mud only to spin to a stall and had eventually given up.

Finally, to our pleas Dad had said, "All right, I'll let you boys try once to get over that slick. If you stall, then back the car down and put it back into the garage."

Uncle Taylor and Dad stood in the barn lot watching. Neither believed we could drive through the deep mud up the steep incline. But we had several advantages in the Model-A over later model cars. The Model-A was lower geared. Also a '30 or '40 model car swung low and the chassis caught in the mud; the Model-A stood high on its large, narrow wheels.

Before we attempted the mud ruts, I told Jim and Jimmy to stand on the rear bumpers, one on each side for extra weight on the drive wheels. Having driven tractors in the fields I knew that traction was more important than speed.

In low gear we made for the ruts. I accelerated at a steady crawl up the grade. The Ford's high wheels climbed the mud bank onto the firm ground on the road above the field. I stopped to let the boys back in. We waved to Dad and Uncle Taylor who stood with their hands in their bib overalls. They waved back, and then we climbed the mountain road. Dad had always been generous with his car.

* * *

I sat at the dining table thinking about Shirley. When driving with her, the four-cylinder engine running clear and smooth as a sewing machine, Shirley would suddenly reach over and press the horn button—*aah uuuga uuga*. She tooted the horn and waved at everyone she knew. I'd give the engine more spark and press the accelerator. There was only one car that made that clear Model-A sound accelerating.

"Mama, what am I going to do?" I asked.

She hung her dishrag on the stove handle and turned to me. "You talked yourself into your mess; you'll have to get yourself out." She took her chair beside Dad before the hearth and began piecing another quilt. Over the top of his newspaper Dad looked at her.

I sat in a straight chair and thought of other days I had been with Dad and the Model-A Ford. Once taking some chickens to the Farmers' Market we had two flat tires. Dad showed me how to change the tires and to patch the puncture in the inner tubes, and to use tire boots for thin tires. During the war years it was common to pass people on the road patching old, worn tires.

Once when Dad took the twins and me to the movies, he parked the car on an Asheville street and as we walked away, Dot said, "That man back there picked up some keys on the sidewalk." Dad had lost them through a hole in his pocket.

Once the Ford was stolen. Uncle Lloyd Plemmons saw it parked on an Asheville street, got Dad, and Dad drove it home to the garage. "It'll stay in the garage tonight," I thought to myself.

Dad had lowered his paper at some point in my reflections and he sat watching me. "I reckon Shirley will be ready by now?" he asked.

"Yes," I said.

"Can you remember to park the car on an incline?"

"Yes."

"Put a big rock in front of a tire so it won't coast off?"

"Yes."

"Don't leave the lights on and run down the battery?"

"Yes."

"Can you behave yourself and watch out for others?"

"Yes."

He handed me the keys.

"Thanks, Dad."

Neighbors in the Night

I parked my '41 Chevrolet coupe at the foot of the steps at the cemetery wall. A bright harvest moon in a star-spangled, October night shone down on us. The old white clapboard church loomed large in the midnight moonlight, but for me it was all romance. I had the most beautiful girl in all of Leicester community beside me in my car, and we had had a heavenly evening at the movies. It was time to walk her home.

The Mehaffeys lived in a small bungalow in a clearing beyond the woods, way above the church cemetery. We were as close to the house as I could take the car. I opened my door and Revonda slipped out under the steering wheel and took my arm.

We had no need for a flashlight—not at least until we reached the trail through the woods which Revonda knew completely anyway. The thirteen concrete steps in the lower wall of the cemetery and the gravel path that climbed straight up the ridge between the tombstones were aglow in the silver moonlight.

On the path we often paused, arm in arm, and read a few names on ornate marble monuments.

"You know that Richard Cansler Morgan and Martha Cole were my grandparents," I said.

"Yes."

"And Ernest and Joseph were Dad's brothers?"

151

"Oh, yes," she said, "and here is Marie Sluder, infant daughter of Bess and Taylor Sluder."

"That's Ruth Anne's twin, did you know?"

"Really, and you have twin sisters!"

"Uncle Ernest had twin girls too," I added.

Revonda pointed across several rows of graves and said, "In the plot with the chain fence, a lot of Mehaffeys are buried."

"What do you think about living up there above this large graveyard?" I asked.

Revonda gave me her pleasant, innocent smile and said, "We have the best neighbors in the world. They don't ever bother us."

Above the cemetery, the path took us through a forest of ancient oaks and maples and dogwoods, the wide path all spangled with moonlight and shadows. We ambled on into her yard and climbed the long set of steps onto the high porch. Though a night light burned dimly in the living room, I lingered a moment at the door. With my back to the dark woods and silent cemetery and my car in the empty churchyard, parting was "very sweet sorrow" indeed.

After descending the high steps, I glanced back at the open front door where Revonda stood in the warm glow of the soft light. Again, she said quietly, "Thanks for a nice evening."

A cloud came over the moon as I walked down the trail in the woods. Though I could not see my feet in the darkness, I could follow the opening in the woods to the cemetery path.

For the first time that night I heard an owl screech and

then the flap of his wings toward some small creature. Cicadas sang in chorus and then stopped altogether as the moon peeped through again. I stopped at the edge of the woods above the graveyard and surveyed the long gravel path that led down the hill through an acre of tombstones. As a cloud shadow floated across the silent church house, a host of ghost stories I had heard from my father all rushed into my head.

He told me that as he walked home late one night past the churchyard, he saw something white rise up and disappear. He had stopped and watched that part of the hillside. It happened again and again and again. He said he wondered if his imagination were getting the best of him, but he decided to go investigate. He had found a newly dug grave and discovered that a sheep had wandered into it and was vainly trying to jump out.

Also Dad had told me that Loren Davis and Tommy Brooks used to sit in the graveyard at night and drink moonshine together. Loren had told that on one pitch-dark night, he stumbled and fell into a newly dug grave. As the grave was deep and he was alone, he just sat down to wait for Tommy to come along.

Later, Tommy was feeling his way through the cemetery when he, too, fell into the open grave. Tommy struggled in vain to climb the cold clay walls. Then from the silence of the dark grave, Loren had said, "You can't get out of here." But Tommy did.

I resolved that I was going to walk slowly down the gravel path just like a man ought. Then I remembered another tale Dad had told.

A group of men sat in a log cabin around an open fireplace late in the night telling ghost stories. One announced that he would not go into a graveyard alone at night for anything. His wife, who had been quilting quietly in the room, suddenly said, "Shame on you. I wouldn't be afraid to go into a cemetery at anytime alone."

The men baited her and dared her to go that very night and drive a tobacco stick into the center of Mr. Gaddy's fresh grave. The stick was about as long as a walking cane and sharp at both ends so it could be driven easily into the soft earth of the new grave. They would retrieve the stick in the morning.

The lady in her long dress walked bravely out into the night to shame the men and to establish that a graveyard in the night was perfectly safe from ghosts. However, the lady did not return home. Eventually, the men, urged on by her husband, lit the lanterns and went together to the cemetery.

There they found the woman dead on the grave. She had indeed stabbed the sharp stick into the center of old Mr. Gaddy's grave, but when she had bent over and plunged the stick into the ground, she had stuck it through her long dress too. Evidently, when she had turned to leave and felt the hem of her dress held firmly, she had died of fright.

I told myself that there was no such thing as ghosts, and in the bright moonlight one could see that all the dead were dead. I heard only my footsteps on the gravel.

I stepped lightly down the path, checking out the shadows of the large monuments as I passed. A small loosened stone rolled past me on down the path ahead. I stopped and turned around to see no one between me and the woods. I walked on wondering if any bony hand might reach out and grab the cuff of my trousers. My heart, for no reason, began to pound loudly in my chest.

Two more stones rolled past me on the gravel. My skin crawled and shivers ran all over my body. I didn't dare look back again. Some silent presence must have disturbed the gravel on the path behind me. I broke into a desperate run, overtook the loose gravel rolling down the path, jumped clear over the thirteen steps in the cemetery wall, and tore into my car. I locked both doors.

When the beams of the Chevy's headlights swept across the still tombstones, the cemetery looked peaceful enough. But I thought, "While their neighbors don't bother the Mehaffeys, they scare the hell out of me!"

MARINE

Farewell to the Mountains

"Lassie, go home," I told her. As usual, she had jumped up from her place on the front porch and had trotted at my heels as I left the house and walked alone down the gravel toward the paved highway a mile away. I meant to catch the Pisgah and Leicester bus to Asheville. I was leaving home.

On Friday I had stood beside Uncle Oliver's Ferguson tractor with Dad on the seat. The plow blades bit deep into the red clay soil. Snowflakes whirled around us in the raw winter wind. Lassie stood looking first at Dad and then at me as we talked.

"Do you want me to plow awhile?" I had asked. Dad's long pause and his look over the field of overturned soil and his patient study of the unplowed land had been answer enough. Dad was enjoying the work. The tractor purred quietly along and the sharp, twin plows turned the soil over smoothly. He really didn't need my help.

"No, I reckon not," he finally said. Then he added, "Can't you find something else to do?"

"I could go down and look at the Reynold's place," I began.

"Now, let's not start that again," he barked. "We're not buying that farm. You're only eighteen and this country's in another war."

"Police action," I corrected.

"Police action or not," he snapped, "you're registered for

the draft, and there ain't nothing to keep you home." But I had one hope. In his presidential campaign, Eisenhower had promised that if he were elected he would end the Korean War.

"I could get deferred if I had a farm to manage," I argued.

"That Reynold's place ain't no 'count. I'd like to buy you a farm but you're not a man yet. A man don't live on pipe dreams."

I knew I could not budge him, but I continued, "I studied agriculture in high school and I can do a man's work any day."

That set him off. "Man's work! You ought to be in the army. They'd make a man of you."

Suddenly, there in the field I made a decision. "I'm going to town," I said.

I turned from the tractor and stumbled across the furrows toward home. Lassie gave a yap at the moving tractor and trotted at my side.

Dad had not been the only one to suggest my leaving home. Uncle Taylor, who had helped me get into the dairy business, had often told me that when I got through high school I ought to go to college. "Amount to something," he had said. "These mountain farms are too small to maintain more than one family. Get out and see the world before you get stuck here in these hills."

I hadn't told Dad and Mom that while I was attending Blanton's Business College I had walked four blocks to the draft board office and asked about my situation. Mrs. Cox had leafed through a wire basket on her desk and found my draft notice. When I told her I was attending business college she told me that college was not sufficient reason to be deferred from the draft. However, she did place my notice on the bottom of the stack and told me that her quota for November would exclude me. I went back to see her in December. When I entered the door she quietly leafed for my form and placed it on the bottom of the stack again. No words passed between us.

As I stumbled over the furrows I thought, "I'll show them. I'll join the Air Force."

It was around noon in Asheville when I walked into the post office and followed the signs to the recruiting offices. I passed up the Army recruiter. The Navy waiting room was full of young men, so I went on to the Air Force recruiter. No vacant seats were there either. Everyone, it seemed, wanted to join the "gentleman's service," but I soon got a seat and waited my turn to talk with the recruiter.

"I can take your name," he said, "and put you on the waiting list."

"How soon can you call me?" I asked.

"The wait is about three months right now." That was not good enough for me, but I let him take my name and address and I walked out. When I saw the Marine Corps poster at the far end of the hallway, I walked down that way. No one was in the office. I strolled in and began to browse through the literature. "Join the Marines and see the world," I read. Presently a recruiting officer returned from his lunch break.

"What can I do for you?" he asked as he stepped into the room.

"Can I join the Marines?"

"I don't see why not." He looked me over.

"How soon can you take me?"

"I can ship you out Monday morning if you qualify." I qualified. All he needed was a birth certificate and a parent's signature. I drove to the shirt factory where Mother worked, waited for her, and took her back to his office.

"If this is what you want" was all she said. She signed the parent consent form and I signed the enlistment papers contingent upon my passing the physical in Raleigh.

At supper that evening I quietly said, "I joined the Marines today and I'll be leaving early Monday morning." Dad just looked at me. "The sergeant said that I'd be examined on Tuesday in Raleigh and if I passed the physical I'd be sworn in and sent to Parris Island for boot camp," I told him.

"Ah," he said with a teasing glint in his eyes, "then you'll be back home on Wednesday, I reckon." He watched me closely and then added, "You won't pass; they want men."

On that Monday morning I took a last look at my '41 Chevy coupe and walked onto the gravel. In the bitter, cold morning air, Lassie stopped and stood wagging her tail, looking up at me with hurt eyes.

"Lassie, go home!" I scolded again and watched her turn back toward the house. I turned and wiped my eyes on my coat sleeve and walked on down the road.

Joe Morgan left the western North Carolina mountains to serve with the United States Marine Corps for four years during and after the Korean conflict. He then earned his B.A. degree in literature at Wheaton College, Wheaton, Illinois. After receiving his M.A. from Illinois State University, he went on to doctoral studies with New York University at York University in Heslington, England.

A teacher who has taught language, literature, and writing for over thirty years, Mr. Morgan has been selected twice by his colleagues as teacher of the year and has received the Illinois Governor's Award for Excellence in Teaching. Since 1970 he has been a consultant for the Illinois Writing Project. By writing the stories in *Potato Branch,* Joe demonstrated for his students how to shape stories, develop characters, and focus on themes from their own life experiences.

Joe has two daughters and a son and lives with his wife, Milli, in Wheaton, Illinois.

APPENDIX

GRANDPARENTS
Joe and Madie Nan Hall Anders
Richard "Uncle Canse" Cansler and Martha Cole Morgan (sister to Gaston and Jasper Cole)

PARENTS
C. C. "Buddy" and Della Anders Morgan

SISTERS AND BROTHER
Dot, Dean, Glennan, and Webb Morgan

AUNTS AND UNCLES
R. D. and Rudy Anders Terry
Oliver and Carrie Jones Morgan
Lloyd and Ruth Morgan Plemmons
Ernest Morgan
Harry and Blanch Plemmons Morgan, parents of Max and Don
Grover and Clora Morgan Roberson, parents of Gwen
Taylor and Bess Morgan Sluder, parents of Ruth Anne
Joseph Morgan
Bud and Estelle Morgan Mehaffey

UNCLE OLIVER'S TENANT FARMERS
Bud Bonnom
Garland Dills
Marshall Gregg
Amos Knight

NEIGHBORS
Fred and Lela Mehaffey Anders (sister to Arthur and Bud Mehaffey)
Mary Anna, Cora Estella, and Mark Daves
Robert and Pearl Robertson